Endorsements

Donna Nabors has provided a beautiful depiction of the grace and power of God to transform a life. In her new book, *Shattered Dreams to Treasured Truths, Transforming Life's Disappointments*, she gives hope to anyone desiring to move forward in peace through forgiveness. You will enjoy this book, I know I did! Get ready to be blessed and fill up your spiritual jewelry box with the blessings of heaven.

> DANNY FORSHEE
> Pastor, Great Hills Baptist Church and President the Danny Forshee Evangelistic Association

Donna is a gifted Bible teacher whose lessons shine like gold on every page of this book. She shares her worst experiences with grace and communicates with confidence that we are equipped, in Christ, for every circumstance This book is, indeed, a gem.

> LORI STANLEY ROELEVELD
> Author of *The Art of Hard Conversations*, speaker, disturber of hobbits
> www.loriroeleveld.com

Donna Nabors speaks a language most people are not familiar with today. She is fluent in transparency. From panic to peace and every emotion in between, she openly shares wisdom when we are at our wits end and leads us to Christ in the crisis. Her book, *Shattered Dreams to Treasured Truths* speaks to broken hearts encouraging the reader to not only die in peace, but to live in peace. It is possible and Donna explains how!

Tammy Whitehurst
Speaker, Author, and Conference Director of the Christian Communicators Conference
www.tammywhitehurst.com

Shattered Dreams to Treasured Truths is written for any woman whose life has taken an unexpected and unwanted turn.

The book is not designed as a tell-all of her ordeal. Instead, she shares her story and trumpets the abundant goodness of God. Nabors sees a victorious pass-through: "Instead of being *transformed by* the negative, I want to look at *transforming the negative,* taking the disappointments we encounter and transforming them through treasured truth."

If life has brought disappointment, this book will reassure you that you are in good company with the women of the Bible—where Donna found her transformation. "It (the Bible) is full of real life, but it doesn't stop short. It doesn't leave us empty. The Bible gives the answers to how we can transform those disappointments and our shattered dreams can be restored."

Deb DeArmond
Multi-Published Award-Winning author including *Don't Go to Bed Angry, Stay Up and Fight*, Writing Coach and Speaker

Shattered Dreams
to Treasured Truths

Shattered Dreams to Treasured Truths

TRANSFORMING LIFE'S DISAPPOINTMENTS

DONNA NABORS

Carpenter's Son Publishing

Published by Carpenter's Son Publishing, Franklin, Tennessee

Published in association with Larry Carpenter of
Christian Book Services, LLC
www.christianbookservices.com

Edited by Ann Tatlock

Cover and Interior Layout Design by Suzanne Lawing

Printed in the United States of America

978-1-952025-80-8

This book is dedicated to Mr. Wonderful.
You are my encouragement and continual support.

Contents

Foreword

When our white picket fence dreams crumble at our feet, sometimes the only thing we can do is sort through the rubble for the gems of truth. That is the hope Donna Nabors offers us in her book, *Shattered Dreams to Treasured Truths: Transforming Life's Disappointments.* Through her writing she gifts us with profound spiritual insight and discernment garnered through a life spent determined to seek God's truth no matter how broken her world seemed at the time.

I've had the pleasure of watching Donna live out the principles she dispenses with candid honesty on these pages. With poignant transparency, sage humility, and oftentimes humorous witticisms, Donna shares real-life experiences—both the good and the bad—in her search for the priceless jewels of understanding that turn shattered dreams into treasured truths.

By combining fascinating facts about the precious gemstones that speak to us of rare beauty with the precious truths of God's love that reveal to us the rare life He offers, Donna reveals a path to genuine riches. From the diamonds of faith to the emeralds of hope, the reader will be blessed with a wealth of fresh perspective.

The book you are holding isn't about the grief of betrayal, abuse, or divorce. It's about seeing God's sovereign hand working in your life. It's about finding the richness and treasures contained in His Word and then learning to polish these gems of faith until they radiate joy, peace, and hope in every facet of your lives.

It's about making His priceless design your treasured truth no matter how shattered your dreams become.

Shattered Dreams to Treasured Truths is a treasure hunt that will enrich your life.

LORI ALTEBAUMER
Author of *A Firm Place to Stand,* Selah Award Finalist

Introduction

I woke up exhausted after a good night's sleep. It happens from time to time, sometimes more often than it should. The world weighs heavy. Panic on the news over fuel shortages which will filter down through the transportation industry to product and food shortages. Grocery stores overrun by panic buying with not only empty toilet paper shelves but empty fresh food shelves including meat, dairy, and produce. It's a recurrence of what has happened before.

This type of panic can stem from real issues, but the panic itself is a result of fear of the unknown. In truth, every day is unknown. We aren't guaranteed tomorrow with our loved ones or in this life.

I've suffered many disappointments in life from trying out for cheerleader with no hope of being selected to a promising marriage ending in divorce to the loss of my parents. No one escapes disappointment. In fact, troubles are guaranteed.

So, what happens when life doesn't turn out the way we plan? What if life's disappointments seem more than we can handle?

The book of Ecclesiastes can be a depressing book to read. It's basically a summary of despair showing the emptiness of life. But at the end, Solomon gives the answer to this despair, and this is where I want to pick up in this book you are about to read.

> "the writing of many books is endless, and excessive study is wearying to the body. The conclusion, when everything has been heard, is: fear God and keep His commandments, because this applies to every person" (Ecclesiastes 12:12-13 NASB).

Psalm 119:11 tells us to hide God's Word in our heart, but we can't hide it if we aren't in it. In the same way, we won't know His commandments if we don't read them.

Scripture tells us we can be renewed, which is to make new again. We are told to renew our mind, that we are renewed by a new birth, and that our inner man needs to be renewed day by day. In each instance, the renewal comes by a transformation from the Holy Spirit through the Word of God. It is never too late for renewal.

My prayer is that as you read parts of my story and the stories of women in the Bible, you will consider your own story and seek the treasures God has for you. I pray you will find transformation in your own life. You CAN live beyond disappointments and shattered dreams.

Wherever you are today, you can step into tomorrow adorned with gemstones of faith, strength, love, peace, and hope.

Part 1
Transforming Life's Disappointments

1

Transformation

Transformation. This word is commonly defined as a thorough or dramatic change in form or appearance. When something is transformed, it is thoroughly changed. No evidence of the original remains. The butterfly is a wonderful example of this transformation. It begins as an ugly caterpillar with seemingly no hope except to crawl on the ground. Then a transformation changes the caterpillar into a beautiful butterfly adorned with vivid colors and wings to fly. It is thoroughly changed.

Change isn't always pleasant. Disappointments, tragedies, heartbreak, grief all bring transformation. We have all had experiences or changes that overwhelm us. The greatest problem with any disappointment is the effect we allow it to have on our life.

Have you ever experienced the pull of the ocean waves? We can be carried out farther and farther into deep waters without being aware until the waves engulf us. If carried out too far, fighting the waves can leave us with little energy to reach the shore. But if we give up, we will only drift out even farther.

Instead of being transformed by the negative, I want to look at transforming the negative. Taking the disappointments we encounter and transforming them through treasured truth.

As we begin this journey, I share in the next chapter about a broken and failed marriage that should have been a representation of the gospel. Instead the marriage brought overwhelming disappointment and, like the treacherous waves of the ocean, depleted the energy of everyone involved. This book is not about the devastation or failure of this marriage. It is about the transformation of failure involving worry, weakness, bitterness, frustration, and discouragement. This change came through faith, strength, love, peace, and hope. These are the treasures of truth we seek and find in Scripture.

I encourage you to read beyond the pain of the next chapter to find new hope amid whatever disappointment you may be living in now or encounter in the future. Just as the caterpillar emerges as a beautiful butterfly adorned with vivid colors, together we will discover our own transformation through our spiritual jewelry box. We will transform our lives by placing diamonds of faith, sapphires of strength, rubies of love, amethysts of peace, and emeralds of hope inside. Then we too will emerge adorned with vivid colors from the treasured truths we find in God's Word and be free to fly.

"And do not be conformed to this world, but be transformed by the renewing of your mind, that you may prove what is that good and acceptable and perfect will of God" (Romans 12:2).

2

Shattered Dreams

My jewelry box represented lies, broken promises, and pain.
Every piece given to me for a special occasion was a lie. Even
the diamonds set in gold encircling the third finger of my left
hand represented a lie.

"With this ring, I thee wed. Wear it as a symbol of my love
and commitment."

Yet there was none.

"This ring is a symbol of my commitment to love, honor,
and respect you."

It might as well have turned my finger green. It was a symbol of indifference. Each sparkle of light reflected from the
center diamond depicted a life of deceit and unfaithfulness.

"With this ring I thee wed, and all my worldly goods I thee
endow. In sickness and in health, in poverty or in wealth, till
death do us part."

It died before it was even born.

My questions were endless. Why? How do I move forward? Where do I go? How do I trust again? How do I forgive? Where do I turn? Why? How? Where? When? Who? What? So many questions. No answers.

I needed faith.

I needed strength.

I needed love.

I needed peace.

I needed hope.

# # #

Weddings are beautiful because they represent a commitment of two lives joined together in love. Though it might be this bride's sentimental memory, mine was taken from the pages of a bridal magazine. It was beautiful. Or was it?

The church was decorated simply with yellow and white ribbons fastened at the end of each pew. Candelabras held white tapered candles intertwined with flowers at the front of the church. Bridesmaids in yellow summer dresses carried small bouquets. My bouquet combined white roses, carnations, and daisies accented with baby's breath throughout.

As my daddy lowered my veil and prepared to walk me down the aisle, I felt a familiar feeling in my stomach as if hundreds of butterflies were about to escape up my throat and out my mouth. Was I doing the right thing? Of course, I was. This was a dream come true. I was about to become a pastor's wife and could not wait to serve God with my new husband. Besides, it was time to walk down the aisle. Why would I question this now?

Breathe in. Breathe out. Release the fluttering inside.

Following my bridesmaids, I walked down the aisle on my daddy's arm to the man I planned to spend the rest of my life with. We pledged our vows to one another promising to love, honor, and cherish, and the pastor pronounced us man and wife. A reception followed the wedding including the obligatory bride's cake with buttercream frosting and white roses, my mother's frozen punch, and finger foods. All was well in my life.

After the reception we changed into casual shirts and shorts and jumped in the car heading to a hotel on the beach where we would spend our honeymoon. My beautiful wedding bouquet of roses, carnations, and daisies rested on a pillow in the back seat. But first, we stopped at a convenience store to pick up a few items.

When we returned to the car, my new husband who pledged to love, honor, and cherish threw a 2-liter bottle of Sprite into the back seat and onto the delicate flowers. I let out a shriek, "The flowers!"

As he watched me climb over the front seat to move the bottle and save the flowers, he said, "It's just a bunch of flowers. It's not a big deal."

My jaw dropped and my mouth fell open as if someone had punched me in the gut. All the butterflies I released earlier flew back into my mouth and down my throat into the pit of my sore stomach.

They were only flowers, but they represented so much more. They represented promises. They represented dreams. They represented the blooms of years to come. I didn't realize it then, but just a bunch of flowers would lead to just a bunch of lies and unfulfilled dreams and years that would never come. As the flowers in the bouquet died, so would the vows that never really lived.

I needed faith.

# # #

Married just over a year, he walked out the door after another argument; but he left his wallet on the kitchen table. Opening the wallet, I discovered a condom tucked behind his driver's license. I was on birth control. There was no reason a condom should be in his wallet. As I stood there questioning what I found, the rattle of the doorknob and the squeak of the back door opening drew my attention. He had returned for his wallet and entered the kitchen where I stood.

I confronted him, and he went into a rage. His arms flailed and his voice raised, "What makes you think you can go through my wallet?" Somehow everything always became my fault. He pushed me against the edge of the kitchen counter between the refrigerator and the stovetop. He grabbed the carving fork from the knife block next to the stove and placed it at my throat. My body began shaking. I thought my pounding heart would leap out of my chest, but deep inside I didn't believe he would go that far.

"Go ahead."

He shoved me harder against the counter pressing the fork tongs against my clammy skin, but then he tossed the fork aside.

"You aren't worth it."

He picked up his wallet and walked out the back door.

I couldn't believe what just happened. It was as if someone struck the back of my knees with a baseball bat. My legs snapped like a rubber band, and I collapsed on the floor alone once again. Relief or disappointment?

I needed strength.

# # #

A year and a half into the marriage, and there was always an argument. I couldn't do anything right. Once again we were fighting, and I didn't even know why. It was all so pointless. Then he pushed me. This time it was more than the normal shove to get out of his way. I stumbled. He pushed me again, and I fell. My weakness in that moment released more of his anger.

I looked up to see fury in his cold, dark eyes. He kicked me. "You are worthless." He kicked me again. As I curled into a ball to protect myself from what might come, he spit on me, told me again that I was worthless, turned, and walked out the door.

I lay on the living room carpet crying. I felt my heart bleeding, but it was an internal hemorrhage of the heart no one else could see. I couldn't remember a single night I hadn't cried since the first week we were married. What had happened? How could this have turned out so wrong? I couldn't even pray. Was I really worthless?

I needed love.

# # #

A year later we bought our first home. We converted the single-car garage into a study, and I enjoyed decorating the house. He was still in seminary, but he was now the pastor of a small church excited about having a young preacher who

25

could bring revival to their congregation and community. I held onto hope as our surroundings changed. I refused to stop believing for healing in our marriage. Ministering to others in a church where he was excited to pastor had to be a path to restoration.

One afternoon I answered the phone at work. Anxiety ate away at my insides as I heard his raised voice on the other end of the line.

"Why didn't you make more iced tea? We are out of ketchup too. Am I going to have to start doing the grocery shopping for you? You can't do anything right."

I wanted to be the perfect wife, and I was failing. Buried deep inside I knew he was unreasonable, but why couldn't I do anything to please him? There was nothing I could say or do. He let me know I had failed again. Really? Would I ever be good enough?

I needed peace.

# # #

Had it only been a few years since my flowers were crushed by a bottle of Sprite and my dreams began to die? I drove home after a long day at work torn between praying his car would be in the driveway and praying he wouldn't be home.

If he were home, I would have to deal with the next onslaught of what I had done wrong or how I never lived up to who I should be. I never knew how mad he would be or what he would do.

If he wasn't home, it meant he was out at the bars or with another woman. My greatest desire was for him to love me and want to be home with me. But when he was home, there was never peace.

The butterflies had left long ago. My stomach curled into a knot as I rounded the corner into our neighborhood. The driveway was empty. A mixture of relief and sadness tore me apart. I couldn't do this anymore.

I needed hope.

# # #

Have you ever needed faith, strength, love, peace, or hope? These were just some of the things I needed. These stories are parts of my first real disappointment in life. A marriage full of promise ending in divorce.

There are also many stories of women's struggles in the Bible. Some were barren or lost children and family. Others were raped. Many risked their lives for God and family. They took care of their homes, had careers, and showed courage. Some made sacrifices of their lives, and there are at least two women listed in Hebrews chapter 11 as women of faith. There is also a host of women we don't see, supporting the men listed in this chapter of faith.

The Bible is realistic. It paints true life stories of worry, weakness, bitterness, anger, and discouragement. If you have had disappointment in life, you are in good company with the women of the Bible. It is full of real life, but it doesn't stop short. It doesn't leave us empty. The Bible gives the answers to how we can transform those disappointments and our shattered dreams can be restored. When our life expectations fall apart, there is still hope.

As we travel through the chapters that follow, we will discover how our worries can transform into faith, our weakness into strength, our resentment and bitterness into love, our frustration and anger into peace, and our discouragement into hope.

3

The Jewelry Box

Sometimes I just need to buy a new pair of shoes.

I manage sales administration at the company where I work. If you're not sure what that means, I'll try to explain. I make sure the sales staff at our company can translate what they have done in the field onto paperwork our operations and accounting departments can understand. This can often be difficult to document. Sometimes at the end of the day, I just need to buy a new pair of shoes.

Have you ever wanted to go shopping after a bad day or week? New shoes, new clothes, and maybe even jewelry to accessorize your new outfit would make next week at the office or home with the kids so much better. We have a lot in common. But I bet if we both went to the same store at the same time after the same bad day, we would buy something totally different.

As individual women with many things in common, we are also different in many ways. We are different ages and sizes. We have different hairstyles, shoes, outfits, and jewelry. While most women carry a purse, what's in each purse will vary based on the woman and the season of life she is in. We may all have a phone in our purse, but those with babies might find a pacifier or diaper inside as well. Women with young children might find toy cars or crayons in the bottom of their purse. A woman with long hair might have hair clips, and a woman visiting her grandchildren might have candy tucked away. My husband today calls me his Swiss-army wife, because when we are out of the house and he needs something, more times than not, it's in my purse.

Contrast your purse to your jewelry box. Every woman has some kind of jewelry box, but they are all different. Yours might be a small musical chest or a large cabinet. It could be anything from a shoebox to a safe deposit box. It might sit on top of your dresser or fill an entire dresser drawer. Each one is as individual as you are. It's that special place you keep your treasures and jewelry.

Consider the most treasured item in your jewelry box. Is it your wedding ring? Is it a necklace with precious stones, a diamond bracelet, or a strand of pearls? Maybe it's something that belonged to your great grandmother, passed down from generation to generation. I have a cheap discount store ring that means a lot to me. The man I am now married to gave it to me when we got engaged before he bought the real one. The sentimental value is worth much more than the ring itself.

Our jewelry boxes hold special treasures, but sometimes they get filled with items that don't even resemble jewelry like broken chains, old clasps, safety pins, straight pins, broken watches, buttons, coins, batteries, and more. Just like our purse, our jewelry box can become a catchall for everything at home. It becomes hard to find the valuable pieces because of the odds and ends taking up space. What's in your jewelry box right now — treasure or junk?

A Special Jewelry Box

Imagine receiving a special jewelry box as a gift. The cover might be gold plated, covered in diamonds, or hand carved. Picture whatever is beautiful to you. As you hold this jewelry box in your lap and carefully raise the lid, the most beautiful music ever played surrounds you. You hear angels singing. Shimmering white satin lines the inside. Precious gemstones—diamonds, sapphires, rubies, amethysts, emeralds—shine against this soft satin background. These jewels reflect perfect light. This isn't just any jewelry box. It's your spiritual jewelry box. Even the smallest stone within represents a treasure God has given you.

As Christian women, our most treasured possession is God's Word, so it only makes sense to place it in our spiritual jewelry box. Our inner adornment comes from what is inside this jewelry box. Scripture tells us that while others see our outward appearance, God sees our heart. We can put all kinds of physical jewelry on the outside to look pretty, but what we put in our spiritual jewelry box is known by God and still ends up reflecting to others on the outside.

Good Enough

I was a shy little girl, almost to the point of being fearful, not wanting to be noticed by anyone I didn't know well. Yet somehow I stepped out into a church aisle one Sunday morning and walked to the front of the church where our pastor stood. I knew I needed what he had talked about.

We all have a different testimony of faith in God. Each one is important and offers encouragement to others. Several years ago I attended a training class at church about sharing our faith. The leader taught us to share briefly what our life was like before Christ, how we came to know Christ and what He saved us from, and then what our life was like after Christ. I thought my testimony wasn't that good. I wasn't saved from a life of drinking, drugs, gangs, or abusive behavior. I was in elementary school. I was a good kid raised in a Christian home. I wanted to please my parents and teachers. I was nice to others and had attended church since the month I was born. What was my life like before Christ? One word — GOOD.

But I knew even at my young age I needed a Savior. I was a sinner. In our world of rating sins, mine weren't that bad. But I was still a sinner. It didn't matter how good I was; I could never be good enough. And that makes my testimony good enough. It's good enough to share with others, because I wasn't. None of us are. I needed Christ as my Lord and Savior.

After I trusted Christ for salvation, my life didn't change dramatically, but it changed in ways I wouldn't realize for years to come. Founding my life on the rock of Christ at a young age would rescue me from a life of shattered dreams later.

During my senior year of high school, a friend introduced me to a young man studying for ministry. He was already working in different roles of service in mission outreach churches. Two years later we married, and he began pastoring a small mission church. I believed I was following God's calling on my life and was excited to start a new chapter as a preacher's wife.

When I married this young man at nineteen, I thought my life was complete. My hopes and dreams for the future were coming true. I looked forward to serving God, helping others, and raising my children in a Christian home.

But nothing was as it seemed. We encountered financial problems, we had poor communication, he developed addiction issues, there was physical abuse, and that led to emotional abuse. One day I woke up and realized everything in my life was a lie. But what about my faith? Was that a lie too, or was it real? My dreams were shattered. My heart was broken. Where was God?

I had tried to make things better on my own. I had tried to be a good wife, but it was never good enough. Just like my testimony of salvation. I couldn't be good enough for salvation, and on my own, I couldn't be a good enough wife either.

I grew up in a Christian home with parents dedicated to service in the church and to raising their children to learn Scripture and have a relationship with Christ. Many of the scripture verses I know today, I learned as a child. During my teenage years I was involved with our church youth group, worked in summer Bible school programs for children, and went on mission trips to share Christ with others. My experiences in my youth gave me a strong foundation.

Enter my spiritual jewelry box. I didn't realize then how filling the jewelry box in my heart as a child would enable me to adorn my life later. It would fill my heart with what I needed to survive when I stepped out of the shelter of my parent's Christian home and my dreams shattered.

Like many young couples, we struggled financially. I worked full time, and he was in school while also serving in a small church with little pay. I was thankful each month as God met our needs. At one point our parent church went through a transition from one bank account to another. The payroll checks were mistakenly paid out of the wrong account, and they all bounced. We had already written several checks against that deposit, which was reversed. It wasn't his fault or my fault. It was a mistake, but it caused a lot of problems and additional stress straightening everything out.

My first husband and I didn't communicate well. We didn't see things the same. He wanted me to handle the finances, yet he wanted them handled his way, but he never could communicate what that way was. I did everything wrong. Even the fiasco with the payroll check that bounced was somehow my fault. I began to believe his lies about my ability as a wife.

There was addiction. I had never heard the term sexual addiction. Today we hear about pornography addiction, mostly related to the internet. There was no internet then. Yes, there were magazines and such, but his addiction went deeper. It was an addiction he acted on. There were multiple acts of infidelity throughout our marriage.

There was abuse. Sometimes I think the physical abuse resulted from the addiction problems. He knew he had a problem and dealt with his guilt by blaming me. When we argued, it was a fight, and it was a fight that turned physical. Some men wake up the next morning after an alcoholic binge and express remorse or send flowers. He woke up the next day, looked at me, and said, "You deserved it."

This became part of the emotional abuse. I was worthless. I couldn't do anything right. It wasn't just a feeling. He told me every day until I began to believe him.

What's Inside?

Proverbs is a book of wisdom. Chapters 2 and 3 of Proverbs discuss specifically its importance. We are to treasure wisdom, seek her as silver, and search for her as hidden treasure. Verse 10 says wisdom enters our heart. And there in our heart, we find our spiritual jewelry box. When my hopes and dreams shattered, I opened mine.

There I found the precious stones providing what I needed to survive.

• When I needed faith, I had diamonds from the Word:

> *"Be strong and of good courage; do not be afraid,*
> *nor be dismayed, for the LORD your God is*
> *with you wherever you go" (Joshua 1:9).*

And just as God was with Joshua, He promised to be with me.

"I will never leave you or forsake you" (Hebrews 13:5).

I was never alone.

"No temptation has overtaken you except such as is common
to man; but God is faithful, who will not allow you to be
tempted beyond what you are able, but with the temptation
will also make the way of escape, that you may be able to bear
it" (1 Corinthians 10:10).

What I couldn't handle alone, I could handle with God.

- When I needed strength, I had sapphires from the Word:

  "My soul melts from heaviness; Strengthen me according to Your word" (Psalm 119:28).

God gave me strength as I looked to His Word.

  "My grace is sufficient for you, for My strength is made perfect in weakness" (2 Corinthians 12:9).

In my weakness, He was my strength.

  "Blessed is the man who trusts in the Lord, and whose hope is the Lord" (Jeremiah 17:7).

As I trusted in God, He became my hope and trust.

- When I needed love, I had rubies from the Word:

  "For God so loved the world that He gave His only begotten Son, that whoever believes in Him should not perish but have everlasting life" (John 3:16).

God loved me so much that He sacrificed His Son for me.

  "We love Him because He first loved us" (1 John 4:19).

God's love made it possible for me to love.

  "Neither death nor life, nor angels nor principalities nor power, nor things present nor things to come, nor height nor depth, nor any other created thing, shall be able to separate us from the love of God which is in Christ Jesus our Lord" (Romans 8:38-39).

Nothing could separate me from God's love. Not anyone or anything anyone could do.

- When I needed peace, I pulled out amethysts from the Word:

  "The Lord is my shepherd . . . He restores my soul"
  (Psalm 23:1, 3).

This reminded me that the Lord will guide me and restore my soul when I am weary.

"You will keep him in perfect peace, Whose mind is stayed on
You, Because he trusts in You" (Isaiah 26:3).

I was reminded to pray because Scripture says God will give me perfect peace when I focus on Him.

"And the peace of God, which surpasses all understanding,
will guard your hearts and minds through Christ Jesus"
(Philippians 4:7).

I knew when I gave up my worry and gave my requests to Him, He alone could give me peace that surpasses all understanding. I can't explain that peace to you. It's true. It surpasses all understanding.

- When I needed hope, I had emeralds from the Word:

"The steadfast love of the LORD never ceases; his mercies never
come to an end; they are new every morning; great is your
faithfulness. 'The LORD is my portion,' says my soul, 'therefore
I will hope in him'" (Lamentations 3:22-24).

He gave me hope, so I could get up each day, one day at a time. My hope was in God, not people.

"For we are His workmanship, created in Christ Jesus

for good works, which God prepared beforehand that we should walk in them" (Ephesians 2:10).

Scripture reminded me God had a purpose for my life.

"... looking for the blessed hope and glorious appearing of our great God and Savior Jesus Christ" (Titus 2:13).

There is a greater hope than this life, and I could focus on the glory to come.

My endless questions. Why? How do I move forward? Where do I go? How do I trust again? How do I forgive? Where do I turn? Why? How? Where? When? Who? What?

One answer. The treasures of truth in my spiritual jewelry box. This is where I found the redemption of my shattered dreams. This is how I would transform life's disappointments.

Adornment

*"Do not let your adornment be merely outward—
arranging the hair, wearing gold, or putting on fine
apparel— rather let it be the hidden person of the heart, with
the incorruptible beauty of a gentle and quiet spirit, which is
very precious in the sight of God" (1 Peter 3:3-4).*

Let's break down the meaning of this scripture.

The word *adornment* means orderly arrangement or decoration. The verse in 1 Peter is the only place in the Bible where the original Greek word is translated as adornment. Other verses translate the same word as *the world*. In other words, it's how you put yourself together.

The word *gentle* means meek or humble.

The word *quiet* means still or peaceable. It can convey keeping one's seat, being immoveable, or steadfast.

In relation to our adornment, I think of it as wearing our jewelry simply stated versus wearing everything in our jewelry box at once.

The word *precious* means of great price, costly, or extremely expensive. The gemstones we consider precious stones are diamonds, rubies, emeralds, and sapphires. These precious stones come at a great price.

Being adorned by God is filling our spiritual jewelry box with everything he has for us, so we can then wear whatever we need for that day or that moment. Simply stated, quietly making an impact.

We each have our own stories with different areas of discouragement, worry, doubt, and fear. We share a need for faith, strength, love, peace, and hope. Circumstances can seem desperate or impossible. We become overwhelmed. Each situation is unique, and our individual experiences make us who we are. I don't know what you are going through right now. No one else may know. You may outwardly appear in control while inside you are falling apart.

We also each have dreams. We want today to be the beginning of a perfect ending. But life can get in the way. What happens when your dreams are shattered? How do you recover when life doesn't turn out the way you planned? How do you overcome disappointments? God doesn't expect us to pretend that disappointments aren't there. He does expect us to bring them to Him so He can guide us through them.

When I was a young minister's wife, no one knew what I was going through. But there is a common factor in how the women in the Bible, how I, and how you too can transform life's disappointments and survive shattered dreams. It's called our Spiritual Jewelry Box. You can continually fill it with rocks of worry, weakness, resentment, anger, and discouragement or you can exchange those rocks for faith, strength, love, peace, and hope. The bottom line is that you can't take out what you need if you haven't placed it there first.

What do you need right now? In the chapters that follow, we will discover how a spiritual jewelry box works, look at steps to filling your own jewelry box, and then dig into the treasures of God's Word together. We will find the faith, strength, love, peace, and hope we long for. But first we need to understand our second nature.

4

Second Nature

At fifteen years old, I sat behind the steering wheel of a simulated driving experience inside a portable building in the parking lot of my high school. We spent a certain number of hours in the simulator as well as studying the driver handbook before earning the privilege to sit behind the wheel of a real car. Four students and one instructor rode in each car. Three students sat in the back seat as we each took our turn at the wheel. Once in the car, each driver would adjust the seat, check the mirrors, and make sure they knew where all the controls were--blinkers, lights, windshield wipers, temperature controls, radio, and most important, the brake. Then each student took a turn driving. We started the car, checked our mirrors again, put the car in gear, and slowly pressed the accelerator to move forward. There were so many things to think about. The fact that I was in control of a vehicle capable of causing grave damage to other property and life was over-whelming and scary.

We began with neighborhood driving and then progressed to the highways. One afternoon I drove down the lanes of a busy highway in Dallas, Texas, trying to look brave, but the traffic made me nervous. There was a tall bridge ahead which provided access from one highway to another. I never liked riding over this particular bridge. Then the instructor told me to take the exit that would take us over this bridge. You have got to be kidding.

As we started up the ramp, my heart beat faster. The palms of my hands became slippery, and I had to wipe them on my pants so I could grip the steering wheel. With a white-knuck-led grip on the wheel and a slight tremor in my voice, I told the instructor, "I don't really like heights. I close my eyes every time my parents drive over this bridge." It would be remiss not to say I scared him as his voice heightened almost as high as the bridge. "Don't close your eyes." I wasn't planning on it. We made it over the bridge, changed drivers, and made it back to the school. Despite the scare I gave my instructor, I passed the class and got my license when I turned sixteen.

During that year and those following, I became more and more comfortable behind the steering wheel. Now I get in the car, push a button, put the car in gear, and drive. I don't think about checking the mirrors, finding the light switch, adjusting the temperature control, or turning on the radio. I do it all without stopping to think. It has become second nature. I can even drive over tall bridges without incident. But bridges over long spans of water still bother me.

In first grade, I learned to read and write. I remember the Big Chief writing tablets with dotted lines and thick pencils that filled my small hand. In third grade I learned to read and write in cursive with smaller lines on the page and smaller pencils (I am sad some schools are no longer teaching cursive). Now my brain reads print or cursive without consciously thinking about it. I don't think about the shape of letters and putting them together to form words. I just read. I just write. There was a time when each of us had to learn the basics of reading and writing. We had to practice until it became second nature.

Throughout my elementary school years, I took piano lessons. I can't remember what I learned first, but I do remember practicing scales, learning theory, playing beginner pieces, advancing to harder pieces, and memorizing music several pages long for recitals and guild competitions. I practiced and played for years until it became second nature. I can't remember not knowing how to read music.

Each time I have started a new job or received a promotion to a position with new responsibilities, I have initially felt a little uncomfortable. Some new positions overwhelmed me. I felt like I was in over my head and might drown. But each time I moved into the job one step and one task at a time. Later I could look back and see how I had progressed. I dug into each new job and learned it until the new became second nature, just like the old.

Today . . .

I have no trouble reading because I do it every day.

I have no trouble driving a car because I do it every day.

I am confident in my position at work because I do it every day.

I can still read music even though I no longer do it every day.

The principle is that of second nature. Second nature is an acquired behavior or trait that is so long practiced it seems innate. It is a habit or tendency so deeply ingrained it appears automatic. I particularly like a definition for English language learners I read in Merriam-Webster that makes it plain.

"Second nature is something you can do easily or with little thought because you have done it many times before."

What is second nature for you? What do you do without thinking? It probably includes reading and driving. It might include baking or sewing or dancing. I hope it's brushing your teeth and using deodorant. For some people, it's sarcasm. It could also be sin. My ex-husband's abusive responses may have been second nature responses learned from his childhood or from others. We all have things we have done so long that we do them without thinking. Second nature can be good or bad.

Second Nature Expectations

In my first marriage I experienced circumstances I never dreamed possible. I had no basis for understanding the situation in which I found myself. Most of us don't understand things we haven't previously experienced. Since I grew up in a home with parents faithful to each other and to their children, in a home that showed love and met our needs, in a home without fighting, my expectations were set for that to be my home when I got married. I never considered anything different and beyond my control. It was my second nature expectation.

So how do we handle life when it doesn't turn out the way we expect? This is the question all of us must answer at some point in our lives. Our second nature expectations are many times what cause life's disappointments.

Experiencing abuse as a young woman barely out of my teenage years rewrote my second nature expectations. I came to understand why many times an abused woman won't leave a dangerous situation. She can no longer trust her expectations. What she believed is no longer true, and it paralyzes her reactions. Stepping out into an unknown with no preconceived expectations appears more dangerous than the abusive situation she is in.

Despite the physical abuse, my emotions were more frightening than anything else. At one point, I didn't want to keep going. I felt trapped. I felt like I couldn't live one more day. I felt like a mouse must feel when toyed with by a cat. I was paralyzed. Alone. As a pastor's wife, I believed there was no one I could tell. I experienced what I never before understood. I now knew what it felt like to not want to live. That feeling scared me more than anything else.

During this time, I turned to God and poured out my heart to Him. At my lowest point, feeling like I couldn't go on, I fell down on my knees one night in my living room and cried out to God. I told Him I couldn't live this way anymore, I couldn't keep going, and I told Him how scared I was. It was then God enveloped me with a peace I couldn't understand but I needed so much. He reminded me of His faith, His strength, His love, His peace, and His hope. By turning to God and the foundation of His Word instilled in me through a Christian home, faithful leaders at my church, and study of Scripture, I survived.

Second Corinthians 1:3-4 says God is the "God of all comfort, who comforts us in all our tribulation, that we may be able to comfort those who are in any trouble, with the comfort with which we ourselves are comforted by God." I clung to this verse. I needed comfort. Like the man in Luke 9:24, I cried, "Lord, I believe. Help my unbelief."

What was instilled in me as a child and teen became my salvation. I had learned to read, play the piano, and drive. Those activities became second nature. I had also learned and memorized truths from Scripture. Today I can read because I do it every day. I can drive because I do it every day. I can still read music, but I can't play the piano as well because I don't play every day. In this same way, I had stopped digging deeper in Scripture and growing as I should because I was wrapped up in how my expectations had turned into disappointments. I had to turn back to God and want to please Him versus wanting to please others and be the perfect wife and have the perfect home. I had to renew what was once a second nature response to live for God and not others or myself.

God has given me more than my second nature expectations. He has given me treasures beyond compare. When my ex-husband shattered the dreams of my expectations, I finally turned to Christ and stopped trying to do it on my own. I could never be the perfect wife, the perfect pastor's wife, the perfect housekeeper, the perfect employee, the perfect mom, the perfect cook, the perfect church lady, the perfect author, the perfect speaker, the perfect anything. And I still can't. That is no longer my goal. God's plan for me starts with pleasing Him and being obedient to what He wants. It starts with the treasures in His Word.

We never want to take God for granted, but the truths in His Word should become second nature in application in our lives just like driving or reading or anything we have confidence in doing. It is possible to survive the road bumps and detours of life when our life manual, the Bible, is second nature to us regardless of our expectations.

You may not have had a scriptural foundation as a child. You may feel like your spiritual jewelry box is empty or just full of rocks. Start wherever you are. If you think it will be hard, then remember learning to drive or play the piano. Watch a baby learning to walk. It's hard. They fall down a lot. They must develop their muscles. But if they don't keep getting back up, they will never learn to walk and then begin to run. After much practice, it is mastered and becomes second nature.

New Beginnings?

While my first marriage ended in divorce, I have now been married for over nineteen years to a wonderful man. We'll call him Mr. Wonderful in this book for clarity. Mr. Wonderful attends school online. He completed his undergraduate degree and is now working on his master's. Due to his varying work schedule and being on-call, he couldn't take many hours at a time. Sometimes he got discouraged and felt like he would never finish. But I reminded him that five years from now will still be five years from now. He could be that much farther along in five years or right where he was in five years.

The days will pass whether or not we do anything with them. Think about where you will be five years from today, one year from today, six months from today, two months from today, next week, tomorrow. What will you do today that will make that difference tomorrow?

My goal, and my challenge to you, is for God's Word to become second nature. Not just a natural response without thinking, not just an acquired behavior or trait, but who I am and who you are. This means daily placing God's treasures in our jewelry box, so we have them in each circumstance that comes our way. I want responding with the truth of God's Word to be as natural as breathing. Filling our spiritual jewelry boxes isn't just memorizing scripture. It's living that scripture so that it becomes second nature.

We begin to pray without thinking, "Oh, I need to pray."

We trust without reminding ourselves to trust.

We read and study the Bible because we can't wait to hear from God.

We love others as God loves us.

We forgive as God forgives us.

You may think, "Great for you, but I can't do that."

You're right. You can't.

Galatians 5:22-23 says, "But the fruit of the Spirit is love, joy, peace, longsuffering, kindness, goodness, faithfulness, gentleness, self-control." This fruit is a natural byproduct of living and walking by the Spirit. We can't love by trying to be loving or have joy by trying to be happy. We can't have any of these things by trying. These are manifestations of the Spirit within us.

First Corinthians 13 describes love. This chapter is not a list of how to have perfect love, but a list of what perfect love looks like. It's not a recipe. It's a result. We receive this love as a fruit of the Spirit. We also manifest the other attributes of the fruit of the Spirit when we are abiding in His Word. We are to abide in Him and His Word. We are to be living in His Word. We are to be filling our spiritual jewelry box. Then we will produce this fruit as our new nature.

Wherever you are today, your shattered dreams can be redeemed, and your life's disappointments can be transformed. You can start again. "This is the day the Lord has made; We will rejoice and be glad in it" (Psalm 118:24). Today, every day, is a new beginning. I will rejoice and be glad.

One of my favorite verses is Jeremiah 18:4, "And the vessel that he made of clay was marred in the hand of the potter; so he made it again into another vessel, as it seemed good to the potter to make." Every time I have messed up what God was forming or someone else has messed things up, He has re-formed me. He is the God of not only second chances, but chances exceeding the numbers we can count. He is not just the author of Plan A, Plan B, or Plan C. His alphabet is infinite, and He is just waiting for us to follow Him, trust Him, and stick with His plan.

When my life collapsed and my dreams shattered, I finally opened my spiritual jewelry box to retrieve the treasures I needed. If I hadn't already discovered them and placed them there, it would have been harder. I might have been bitter. I might have given up. Instead, I found calm in the midst of anger, I found hope instead of discouragement, and I found faith instead of worry. I accepted God's love instead of harboring resentment, and He gave me His strength in my weakness.

If I have any regrets, it would be the times women asked me how I could handle situations without falling apart or how I could be strong or why I wasn't bitter, and I failed to share with them God's treasures.

Has God's Plan A for your life been messed up? Do you need Plan B or maybe C or D or even Q or Z? Start with acknowledgement. Acknowledge and admit the sin in your own life. Romans 3:23 says we have all sinned. Acknowledge and recognize the consequences of sin. Romans 6:23 says the consequences of our sin is death, but God has a gift for us through Jesus Christ. Acknowledge and accept this gift. Romans 5:8 explains the gift of God's love by Jesus dying for our sins. And last, acknowledge and confess Jesus Christ as your personal Savior and Lord. Romans 10:9-10 tells us salvation comes from believing in His resurrection and confessing Him as Lord.

If your spiritual jewelry box is new or even if it's older but almost empty or full of dirty rocks picked up on the wrong paths, start today by asking God to help you fill it with His Word.

Sometimes You Have to Dig

Several years ago, Mr. Wonderful and I took a trip to Arkansas and stopped at the Crater of Diamonds State Park. It had rained for several days before, so it was sneaker-sinking muddy and chilly the day we were there. We rented buckets, shovels, and screens and learned how to screen for diamonds. I would love to say we found several large diamonds, paid off our house, and soon retired from our jobs. But that didn't happen.

As we walked the diamond fields of mud, a clear shiny object glistened up at me. I was sure I had found a diamond right on top of the ground, which they told us was possible after the recent rains. When I had it looked at by the experts, we discovered it was a beautiful piece of glass. Of course, that would have been too easy. Most people have to dig to find the real treasures. Few people will stumble upon such treasure without getting a little dirty. Although we didn't find any diamonds, we did get dirty. We enjoyed the experience and had fun learning the process.

Most things in life that are worthwhile are like looking for diamonds. They take time and effort. They take commitment and determination. And sometimes, most times, you need to dig.

Precious gemstones, like diamonds, are mined from the earth and must be cleaned, cut, and polished. They don't just appear on top of the ground ready to place into a jewelry setting. Time and effort are involved. The same is true for spiritual jewelry. It also takes time and effort. There isn't a spiritual jewelry store where you can make purchases after someone else has done the work. Sometimes you have to dig for treasure, but the benefits of the time and effort spent mining for God's treasure are always worth it. You won't come away empty-handed when you dig for hidden treasure in His Word.

Since our spiritual jewelry box doesn't automatically have treasures within, what we place inside is up to us. It will contain either the gemstones we have personally dug from God's Word or stones of worry, pride, anger, self-sufficiency, and other items sought apart from God. When we neglect our relationship with God, we stop receiving new treasures from Him. Are you filling your spiritual jewelry box with treasures from Scripture or with treasures from this world instead?

Is It Second Nature for You?

Making God's Word second nature is an ongoing pursuit. Rate yourself on the following with 1 as never and 10 as always.

1. When I don't understand or wonder why, I continue to have faith in God's plan.

2. When I get knocked down, I look to God first for His strength to get up again.

3. When I am hurt, I respond with the love of Christ because of His love for me.

4. When pressure mounts and I am pulled in multiple directions, I still have unexplainable peace.

5. When I encounter failure, I have an assurance of hope for the future.

How did you do? Maybe it's time to break out your shovel and pick and dig into God's Word.

As we discover gemstones to fill our spiritual jewelry boxes in the coming chapters, we will see they each have their foundation in Scripture. We will dig them from the pages of Scripture and apply them to our life experiences.

Many gem mines no longer allow you to dig on your own. They provide buckets of gem dirt and a screen for washing the dirt away. I pray the pages that follow will help provide a screen for your buckets of gem dirt.

Let's start digging together. Some of the tools we will use can be found in the game of hide and seek in the next chapter.

5

Hide and Seek

My son was three years old, and he didn't want to stay in bed. His four-year-old sister was asleep in the top bunk, but not him. Sitting on the couch, I heard the creak of their bedroom door opening and turned to see him rounding the corner from his room and crawling down the hallway. As I caught his eye, he turned his head. If he couldn't see me, he reasoned that I couldn't see him. He was hiding in plain sight as he crept down the hall with his head turned. I played along. After several minutes, he reached the couch where I was sitting and crawled up in my lap. Even though he was hiding as he crept down the hall, his goal was to be in my arms and not in bed.

When my children were young, we played hide and seek. They would hide, and I would seek. Sometimes I would hide, and they would seek. At first I was easy to find. I might step behind a door leaving it open a few inches with my foot showing. They would be so excited to find me. As they grew older,

I had to make it more challenging. I might hide in a closet, but I would leave the door cracked as a clue. Finally I stopped leaving clues, but they always found me.

Fast forward to grandchildren. I hid so well once, they couldn't find me. Then I decided to sit on the upstairs couch. When one of my grandsons returned, he was amazed, assuming I had been there all along in plain sight. I must have turned invisible for a time.

The same is true for the treasures God has placed in His Word. Some are easy to spot. Some are hidden in the context. Others take more study, but they can all be found. This is why we can read the same passage of scripture several times and each time seems new. Why hadn't I seen that treasure before? It was hidden in plain sight until I grew up enough or needed it enough to see it. And the goal is always to end up in God's arms.

Let's dig in and seek the hidden treasures in Scripture. We are going on a hunt for faith, strength, love, peace, hope, and so much more.

There are three steps to filling our spiritual jewelry box. We seek, we hide, and we keep.

Seek

The treasures for our spiritual jewelry box are already hidden in scripture. We must seek them.

"If you seek her as silver and search for her as for hidden treasures; then you will understand the fear of the Lord and find the knowledge of God" (Proverbs 2:4-5).

"The fear of the Lord is the beginning of knowledge"
(Proverbs 1:7).

Psalm 119 is a great place to start. This chapter has 176 verses, and 171 of those reference God's Word as His law, testimonies, ways, precepts, statutes, commandments, judgments, or words. The psalmist refers to seeking God or keeping His Word with his whole heart six times. He references life from God's Word sixteen times. We can sum up this chapter to say God's Word is what gives us life. Everything we need for a fully redeemed life is there. We must seek with our whole heart because our heart is where our spiritual jewelry box is kept. It is where the treasures we find in God's Word are hidden.

Psalm 119:2, "Blessed are those who keep His testimonies, Who seek Him with the whole heart." The word *seek* means to tread or beat a path, go to a place, frequent, or to apply oneself to any one thing. It is the same word translated search in Jeremiah 29:13, "And you will seek Me and find Me, when you search for Me with all your heart."

Late one afternoon I was sitting behind my desk getting ready to leave for the day when Mr. Wonderful called. As I talked to him, I straightened my desk and prepared what I needed to start working the next morning. Then I gathered my purse and looked for my cell phone. There were only two places it could be, on my desk or somewhere in my purse, but I couldn't find it anywhere. After looking several times in both places and cleaning out most of my purse, I told Mr. Wonderful I was still looking for my cell phone so I could leave. He was confused. Since I was sitting at my desk, I thought I was talking on my desk phone at work, but he had called my cell phone. I was frantically searching my desk and the deep recesses of my purse looking for something that I was holding next to my face. Once I realized what had happened, I felt rather foolish. Mr. Wonderful loves to tell this story.

Have you ever searched wholeheartedly for something? You probably returned to the same places over and over to make sure you hadn't missed it. You might know the last place you saw it and go back there to search again and again. You apply yourself to finding that one thing. This is the way Scripture tells us to seek God. We know He can be found in Scripture; therefore, we should return there over and over. We must apply ourselves to finding Him through His Word and beat a path there often. This is where we find the treasures for our spiritual jewelry box.

Every year when my children were young, I hid Easter eggs for them to find. The joy they expressed as they found each one was precious. My daughter was two years old the first time she understood what she was doing. After she found the last egg, she kept saying, "More, more." This is a great picture of us as children of God seeking the hidden treasures in Scripture. There is joy each time we find another precious stone, and we cry out to God, "More, more." When we are digging into His Word, we can't get enough.

Hide

Once we seek and find what is hidden, it's then our turn to hide. Psalm 119:11 says, "Your word I have hidden in my heart, That I might not sin against You." The word *hidden* used here means to hide, treasure, or store up. God's words are hidden, treasured, and stored up in our heart so we have His treasure to help keep us from sinning. This same word *hidden* is used of Moses. When Moses was born, his mother hid him three months. Scripture again uses the same word of Rahab when she hid the spies. In both instances, these women hid someone to protect them. We place the treasures of God's words in our spiritual jewelry box for protection.

When a tornado or a storm comes, we hide in a safe place. We look for the best shelter for protection. In my house, we gather underneath the stairs in the center of the house. We don't hide so the tornado won't find us, but for protection if it does.

We now see signs in mall parking lots reminding us to hide our valuables. Hide your valuables, lock your car, take your keys. These signs are placed there for our protection.

Jewelry boxes can also be made to hide our valuables. Some are enclosed inside a mirror. I have seen advertisements for fake cans or frozen food containers that can hide valuable jewelry. Have you ever hidden jewelry because of its value? You will wear the jewelry, but you don't want anyone to find and take it. John 10:5 tells us that the thief (the devil) comes to steal, kill, and destroy. He wants to steal our faith, strength, love, peace, and hope. We don't want him to steal from us. So we hide these things in our heart to protect them.

"Do not let your adornment be merely outward—arranging the hair, wearing gold, or putting on fine apparel— rather let it be the *hidden person of the heart*, with the incorruptible beauty of a gentle and quiet spirit, which is very precious in the sight of God" (1 Peter 3:3-4, emphasis mine).

Keep

> *"Keep your heart with all diligence, for out of it*
> *spring the issues of life" (Proverbs 4:23).*

We seek to find, hide, and then keep. Throughout Psalm 119 the psalmist refers to keeping God's Word. When I think of keeping God's Word, I automatically think it means to do God's Word. I think of the Ten Commandments. I think of what scripture tells me to do—love others, be kind, do good. But our English word *keep* can mean many things depending on the context. It can convey the meanings to save, possess, preserve, hide, store, or tend. There are two Hebrew words used for keep in Psalm 119, *shamar* and *natsar*. They have similar meanings: to keep, guard, observe, give heed, or watch over.

In Genesis, God placed Adam in the garden and told him to dress and keep it. To dress it was to work. To keep was to have charge over. The word used in Genesis is the Hebrew word *shamar*.

Keeping a garden involves work. The soil must be prepared, holes dug for planting, roots protected, seeds and plants watered and fertilized, weeds pulled, growth monitored, and pruning done when needed. While there weren't any weeds in the original garden, God told Adam to keep it. He was placed in charge of the care of the garden. This was his work.

Just one chapter later, man was removed from the garden. Cherubims and a flaming sword were placed to keep (same Hebrew word shamar) the way of the tree of life. They were placed to guard, watch, and protect it.

More than just keeping God's Word as in doing it, we are called to keep it in our heart in the context of responsibility. We are charged to guard, watch over, and protect it. Think about a keeper of a garden, a keeper of sheep, and then a keeper of the Word. Protect it from slander and from being used falsely.

Hiding the word and keeping the word go hand in hand. As we are hiding (keeping, guarding, and protecting) God's Word in our heart, it is in turn keeping, guarding, and protecting us from sin.

Beauty from Within

There are four gemstones referred to as precious stones: diamonds, rubies, sapphires, and emeralds. Part of why a stone is considered precious is the Mohs hardness rating, the ability to resist abrasion or scratching. On a scale of 1–10, diamonds are a 10, rubies and sapphires are a 9, and emeralds are an 8. These stones are the hardest and most resistant to scratching.

The precious stones from Scripture protect us. God has given us what we need to stay strong and resist abrasion. Some days we need faith, some days God's love and healing, and some days strength. Other days we need peace and some days hope. What we put into our spiritual jewelry box is what we can then take out and wear. God's precious stones give us what we need. But remember that sometimes, most times, we have to dig into Scripture for them.

Which of these gemstones do you need now?

Redemption

When I was young, I helped my mom fill books with green stamps she received for purchases at the grocery store. Once the books were full, we could redeem them for different gifts. We would exchange our books of stamps for a gift depending on how many books we had. I don't remember the redemption as much as I do licking those stamps and placing them in the books, but my mom enjoyed the redemption.

In Exodus the firstborn of the Israelites experienced re-demption by the spreading of the blood of the lamb on the doorpost. The life of the lamb in exchange for their life. This was a picture of future redemption. Our greatest redemption is Christ dying on the cross in our place in payment for our sins. He exchanged His life for ours. He paid for our gift.

When my dreams shattered, God stepped in and reminded me of His promises. He took the irreparable and made it new. He opened my jewelry box and brought out the treasures I needed and added more. Through His Word, He redeemed my shattered dreams with treasures of truth.

The Bible describes heaven as having streets of gold and walls of precious stones. John describes his vision of the new Jerusalem in heaven.

"And he carried me away in the Spirit to a great and high mountain, and showed me the great city, the holy Jerusalem, descending out of heaven from God, having the glory of God. Her light was like a most precious stone, like a jasper stone, clear as crystal. The construction of its wall was of jasper; and the city was pure gold, like clear glass. The foundations of the wall of the city were adorned with all kinds of precious stones: the first foundation was jasper, the second sapphire, the third chalcedony, the fourth emerald, the fifth sardonyx, the sixth sardius, the seventh chrysolite, the eighth beryl, the ninth topaz, the tenth chrysoprase, the eleventh jacinth, and the twelfth amethyst. The twelve gates were twelve pearls: each individual gate was of one pearl. And the street of the city was pure gold, like transparent glass" (Revelation 21:10-11, 18-21).

Can you imagine the value placed on a physical jewelry box filled with jewels including diamonds, rubies, sapphires, and emeralds? In the same way, imagine the value of a life that reflects spiritual treasure when your heart is full. Filling our spiritual jewelry box gives us a taste of heaven here on earth. Open your spiritual jewelry box. Is it empty, is it full of rocks, or does it have the precious stones you need to follow God's path for your life?

Our Examples

As far back as the giving of the law in the Old Testament, God commanded that His Word should reside in our heart. "And these words which I command you today shall be in your heart" (Deuteronomy 6:6). The verses following in-structed that after placing the Word in their heart, they were to teach it and talk about it all the time--when they walked, lay down, and rose up. They were to bind the words visibly on their bodies and write about them on the doorposts of their houses. We should welcome the opportunity to do the same. This is not just wearing physical jewelry with a cross or hanging scripture verses on the walls of our homes. It doesn't mean we have to get scripture tattoos. This is wearing the Word in our lives where others can see it. It is the outward adornment of what is in our heart.

Paul mentored a young man named Timothy who grew up in a home where he learned Scripture.

"Then he came to Derbe and Lystra. And behold, a certain disciple was there, named Timothy, the son of a certain Jewish woman who believed" (Acts 16:1).

"I call to remembrance the genuine faith that is in you, which dwelt first in your grandmother Lois and your mother Eunice, and I am persuaded is in you also" (2 Timothy 1:5).

"... from childhood you have known the Holy Scriptures, which are able to make you wise for salvation through faith which is in Christ Jesus" (2 Timothy 3:15).

I still know the Bible verses I learned as a child. There were biblical foundations instilled in me as a child, just like Timothy.

Paul reminds Timothy how Scripture was given by inspiration of God and why.

"All Scripture is given by inspiration of God, and is profitable for doctrine, for reproof, for correction, for instruction in righteousness, that the man of God may be complete, thoroughly equipped for every good work" (2 Timothy 3:16-17).

Doctrine shows us God's path for our lives. Reproof exposes when we get off the path. Correction brings us back to the path. Instruction in righteousness keeps us on the path.

If Scripture is given to us as a path for life, we need to know it in order to know our path. Psalm 119:105 says, "Your word is a lamp to my feet, And a light to my path."

Which precious stones have you discovered recently from God's Word? The jewels of this world cannot compare to the riches of Scripture. Make it a goal to spend time digging in God's Word. Search for treasure so your heart will be full and your countenance will reflect God's light to others. True beauty comes from within as we fill our spiritual jewelry box. Let's start filling.

In the second part of this book, we will focus specifically on five gemstones:

Diamonds of Faith

Sapphires of Strength

Rubies of Love
Amethysts of Peace
Emeralds of Hope
The end of each chapter provides a challenge to dig and fill on your own.

Part 2
Filling Your Spiritual Jewelry Box

Diamonds of Faith

Introduction

A typical Wednesday night for a pastor's wife. I was supposed to be at home, and my husband was supposed to be at the mission church he pastored in west Dallas. The church was small, made up mainly of children from our bus ministry and the elderly. We ministered to their needs, hoping to also reach their families. I worked full time in addition to his part-time pastorate while he attended seminary in Fort Worth. Because my job was in Fort Worth, I couldn't make it to the Wednesday night services in Dallas by 6:00 p.m., not to mention it wasn't safe for me to drive into that part of town alone. But this Wednesday night I was not at home. And my pastor husband was not at church.

I discovered investigative skills I never knew I possessed through a sequence of what I will call research episodes. I found out that he had canceled Wednesday night services because of the dangerous area where the church was located.

Instead, he would hang out in a bar on the southwest side of
Fort Worth while I thought he was at church in west Dallas. I
learned from a woman I didn't know that he was at this bar every Wednesday night. It was one more deception in a long line
of deceptions occurring more and more. So this Wednesday
night I drove to southwest Fort Worth and walked into that
bar. I was twenty-two years old and had never been inside a
bar. I know, unbelievable, but true.

Stepping inside, I scanned the room. It only took a minute
to spot him drinking a beer at a table close to the door with
several women. I can't say it hurt or stirred anger. It was sur-
real. He didn't see me. Well, he wasn't exactly expecting me. I
mustered a confident face, and with trembling legs I walked
over to his table, picked up his beer, and poured it down the
front of him. A few gasps; then he stood and marched out. I
followed close on his heels. In retrospect, I should have stayed
and continued my newfound investigative skills. But I left. I
wasn't there for them. I was there for him, fighting for anything left of my marriage.

I don't know what I expected. Remorse? Guilt? Sorrow? An
apology? An explanation? Whatever I expected, it wasn't what
I got. He started his car, and I ran and started mine. He sped
like crazy around other cars in the parking lot, and I followed
as close as possible. I did my best to keep up. I just wanted
answers. Not knowing where he was headed, it was surprising
when he went home. Thinking back, I guess the most logical
place for him to go would be home to change clothes. Wearing
a shirt soaked with beer probably wasn't too comfortable.

I don't remember the exact words said in our conversation,
but I remember it was my fault. No mention of his canceling
church services, no mention of his lies, no mention of his se-

crecy. I was wrong. I messed up. I shouldn't have gone there. How could I do that? How could I embarrass him? It was none-of-my-business. End of discussion. I knew not to push any harder. He didn't leave that night, but I was still alone.

Alone and confused. Who could I talk to? Who could I tell? Who could I ask if I was the one wrong in this situation? He lied. He was out with other women. But I was wrong? He kept me confused. The situation always turned to what I had messed up and my failure as a wife. He expressed no remorse, no sorrow, and no culpability in any of this. My only hope, my only confidante, my only friend—not that diamond in my wedding ring—it was Jesus.

We must first establish faith in our heart in order to transform our disappointments in life. Your disappointments look different than mine, but we all have them. We find diamonds of faith when we firmly plant ourselves in the facets of our faith and Jesus becomes our best friend.

6

Facets of Faith

"Be strong and of good courage; do not be afraid,
nor be dismayed, for the Lord your God is
with you wherever you go" (Joshua 1:9).

"Look at the size of that rock!" Perhaps you've heard this exclamation regarding a large diamond someone is wearing.

When my husband of nineteen years (Mr. Wonderful) proposed, he gave me a ring from a prize machine at a local discount store. It was a symbol, just like a genuine diamond. He knew me well and wanted us to pick out the perfect ring together. I don't wear the prize machine ring, but I have it tucked into a special place in my jewelry box. It wasn't large or expensive. Some would consider it trivial, but it represented his love.

When my children were eleven and thirteen, they had $20 to go shopping for Mother's Day. The department store at the mall had a sale on rings for $10, so they each bought one. They came home with two beautiful diamond rings. Well, two audacious, over the top, something totally out of character for me, diamond rings. The diamonds weren't real, but my children's love for me was. They wanted to buy something beautiful and significant for their mom. I also have those diamond rings in my jewelry box. I don't wear them, but they remind me of my children's love. The fake diamonds themselves may not last forever, but the love they represent will.

The diamonds in my physical jewelry box, whether real or fake, represent the love of Mr. Wonderful and my children. They also remind me of the diamonds in my spiritual jewelry box. Those diamonds represent much more. They lay a foundation for life based on faith in God's Word. I have discovered both small and large diamonds, and each has a purpose in my faith walk with God. Let's use the facets of these diamonds to explore the foundations of our faith.

Diamond Facets

Diamonds have facets, and so does our faith. Scripture references the manifold wisdom of God. The word manifold means many and various, manifesting itself in a great variety of forms. There are many facets of our faith because of the manifold, many-faceted wisdom of our God.

The facets of a diamond are made up of the smooth surface areas which are cut, polished, and positioned at different angles allowing light to enter and reflect from the stone. These facets are a major factor in the diamond's ability to reflect light and play a large part in the resulting brilliance of the stone. Simply stated, the facets produce the sparkle in a diamond.

The facets of our faith are also made up of areas in our lives which have been cut, polished, and positioned, giving us the ability to reflect light and sparkle. There are two key facets of our faith I want to explore. The first is our faith as a noun, our set of beliefs, which we will see in a diamond's value. The second is our faith as a verb, the action we take because of those beliefs. This is like a diamond's reflection because our actions reflect our beliefs.

A Diamond's Value

We value diamonds based on the 4 C's: cut, clarity, color, and carat. Our faith is similar.

- The cut is conviction.
- The clarity brings confession.
- The color leads us to the cross.
- The carat gives confidence.

Learning the 4 C's of our faith gives us the foundation for diamonds in our spiritual jewelry box.

Cut and Conviction

Cut refers to the arrangement of a diamond facet. The cut can be deep, shallow, or ideal. A diamond with an ideal cut captures and releases the maximum play of light. The cut determines how it shines. It doesn't refer to the shape of the diamond.

The cut of our faith is the conviction of sin. Scripture says we all have sinned and will be convicted of sin (Romans 3:23 and John 16:8). There are no grades of sin with God. Because we are all in the same sin box, God's solution was for Christ to pay the price for our sin.

Accepting Christ's payment allows God to shine through our circumstances, reflecting His light even through the tough times. It all begins with the Holy Spirit's conviction. He brings to light an ideal cut.

Clarity and Confession

Clarity is the degree to which tiny marks of nature, called inclusions, are not present in a diamond. Clarity is a measurement of the blemishes (external flaws) or inclusions (internal flaws) a diamond contains.

God's Word brings clarity as we acknowledge our blemishes and realize Christ can wash them clean. The result is confession.

Confession is agreeing with God about our blemishes. We repent of our sins; but what, or who, do we confess? I think everyone knows they sin, even if they don't want to call it that. Even Satan believes (he knows) that Christ died and rose again. The difference is in confessing Christ as our Lord and trusting Him for our salvation.

Color and the Cross

A diamond's color can range from colorless (the rarest and most valuable) to yellow, brown, blue, or red. The color is produced from chemical impurities in its composition. The whiter or more colorless the diamond, the more brilliant because it allows the maximum light to pass through.

Our responses to the cuts in our life have a lot to do with color. Sin places a blemish on our life and inhibits the light of God from shining through. Isaiah 1:18 says our sins are like scarlet red. But once Christ's blood washes away our impurities, we become white as snow. He turns us into a spotless, unstained diamond. Psalm 103:12 says God removes our transgression as far as the east is from the west.

The brilliance reflected in our unstained color comes from the cross of Christ and the blood He shed suffering in our place.

Carat and Confidence

A diamond's size is measured in carat weight. The price of diamonds goes up exponentially for diamonds with a larger carat weight.

Our carat of faith is confidence because of our redemption in Christ. He is bigger than any problem or disappointment in life. He paid the price for our salvation with the ultimate and final sacrifice. Jesus Christ accomplished what we could not do for ourselves, our redemption from the stains and blemishes of sin. We have confidence through faith because of God's promises in His Word to us.

The book of 1 John tells us "these things were written that you may know." We don't have a blind faith. We have God's Word to substantiate it. In daily life, where do you place your confidence? Is your trust in your husband, your finances, your job, your church, or something else? Christ provided our redemption. We can stand firm on our foundation of faith with confidence. This is a BIG carat!

We may have many diamonds in our jewelry box, but they each have different facets depending on the experiences we have had. With diamonds of faith, our fear can now reflect trust. Our weakness can now reflect strength. Our loneliness can now reflect a loving relationship with Christ. Our unbelief and worry can now reflect peace. Our disappointment and discouragement can now reflect hope.

The transformation of life's disappointments become memories reflecting faith for our future.

A Diamond's Reflection

The second facet of our faith is action reflecting our beliefs which stems from our memories. We all have memories. Some may be insignificant in the overall scheme of life, but they are part of what makes us who we are. Memories bring back the past, whether it was an hour ago, yesterday, or fifty years ago. They elicit feelings of thankfulness or regret. Women are often accused of having a significant memory when it comes to what men have done wrong. But there is one who forgets our wrongs. God removes our sins as far as the east is from the west and remembers them no more (Psalm 103:12).

What do you remember?

Remember when phones had cords connected to the wall? I would lie on the floor in my parents' room between the bed and the wall to talk on the phone in private.

Remember when there was a knob on the TV for changing channels? I sat on the floor in front of the set. This made it easier to get up and change the channel. Who knew about the remote of the future?

Remember when texting was done by the number corresponding to the letter you wanted? I remember pressing the number 7 four times for the letter s. My kids could text with the phone in their pocket. What a clever way to text during class and not get caught.

Remember when internet access was through a dial up connection? I remember a dial tone on my computer when connecting to email with the familiar voice of "You've Got Mail" when I received an email. How long ago the days when I looked forward to receiving email.

Remember when commercials were mandatory? Okay, I still enjoy some of today's commercials. That's the best part of the Super Bowl each year.

I also remember getting in trouble as a child and then my mom's embrace of forgiveness. I remember past jobs, saving moments, and answered prayers. If you don't remember something, others do it for you. They share memories through "throwback" moments on social media.

You may not remember the exact things I mentioned, but similar memories are there. In the same way, you probably have memories of what God has done in your life. If not, that's okay. God always comes through, and Scripture has them for you. We have Joshua's memories. We have David's memories. We have Paul's memories. We also have countless other memories recorded for us in scripture.

Joshua had a throwback moment in Joshua 1:5 when God said, "As I was with Moses, so I will be with you. I will not leave you nor forsake you." Joshua remembered Moses' example of following God's leadership, past miracles, and God's provision. He had a reference point to trust God because just as He had been with Moses, He would be with Joshua.

One of David's throwback moments was when he stood before the giant Goliath. He remembered God's provision when he killed the lion and the bear. "The Lord, who delivered me from the paw of the lion and from the paw of the bear, He will deliver me from the hand of this Philistine" (1 Samuel 17:37).

Paul remembered where he came from and that it was God's strength that brought him to where he was. "If anyone else thinks he may have confidence in the flesh, I more so: circumcised the eighth day of the stock of Israel, of the tribe of Benjamin, a Hebrew of the Hebrews; concerning the law, a Pharisee; concerning zeal, persecuting the church; concerning the righteousness which is in the law, blameless. But what things were gain to me, these I have counted loss for Christ ... that I may gain Christ" (Philippians 3:4-8).

Scripture is full of throwback moments. In fact, in many ways all Scripture is a throwback to the past that gives us faith for today and hope for tomorrow. God gave us these stories for our learning and to equip us for life. When disappointments come, we can stand with the psalmist in Psalm 42:6, "My soul is cast down, therefore I will remember You."

Our facets of faith include what God has brought us through and done for us in the past, which influences what we believe now and then affects what we believe about our future.

During my first marriage, I had no point of reference for what I was going through. Before getting married, my life had been uneventful in the problem category. I didn't have the memories of God bringing me through a similar crisis to rely on for faith. But I did have examples from Scripture tucked like diamonds into my spiritual jewelry box. Lots of Bling! tucked in there. Joshua and Caleb were faithful, but the other ten spies were not. They were the sole two who entered the Promised Land. God is always faithful to His promises. Bling!

The book of Hosea tells the story of his unfaithful wife, Gomer. Yet God took care of Hosea. Bling! Delilah betrayed Samson, yet God used Samson. Bling!

Throughout the Psalms, David writes about those who have come against him, but God delivers him through it all. In my Bible the chapter heading of Psalm 55 is Trust in God Concerning the Treachery of Friends. There are many Psalms about David's enemies, but this one is about someone who was once a dear friend. Even then, God sustained him. Bling!

Peter and Judas denied Jesus (one we forgive, but the other we don't--because we know the endings). Jesus died, but He rose again and brought salvation. Bling! And while we might not have the ability to forgive a Judas in our life, Christ did. Bling!

It is imperative to place the treasures of Scripture in our hearts, so we have it at a moment's recall when we need it for example or encouragement. The Bling! of diamonds tucked into our jewelry box helps us remember.

The Faith of Rahab

In Joshua chapters 2 and 6 we read the account of Rahab, a prostitute who lived in Jericho. Joshua sent two men to spy out the land, and Rahab let them stay at her house. When the king of Jericho sent someone looking for these spies, she hid them and sent the king's men on a wild goose chase. She then went to the Israelite spies she had hidden and confessed her belief in their God.

Joshua 2:11 says, "… for the Lord your God, He is God in heaven above and on earth beneath."

Rahab requested kindness and deliverance from the spies when they came back to overtake Jericho, which she knew they would. She helped them escape and gave them instructions on how to avoid their pursuers. They promised to spare her and her family.

Can you imagine being in this situation? She was a prostitute, but she made the decision to trust in God. She helped the spies escape, and they promised to spare her and her family. Rahab had no point of reference to believe these men would honor their word except the stories she had heard about what God had done and who their God was. She believed. She had faith. Then she instructed them to wait three days before returning to their camp.

The spies hid out those three days and then returned to Joshua. After three more days, the Israelites crossed the Jordan. After crossing the Jordan, the second generation of Israelites were circumcised. Joshua 5:8 tells us they stayed in their camp until fully healed. Research shows full healing from an adult circumcision could take from ten days to three weeks. I asked Mr. Wonderful how long he thought it would take to heal. He said a lifetime. I'm glad they didn't wait that long.

Sometime afterwards Joshua encountered the Commander of the Army of the Lord, and the next morning they went out to march around Jericho. It could have been a month after the spies left Rahab before they began their march around Jericho.

I imagine Rahab watched for their return every day. After a week, her faith might have begun to waver. I waver after a day sometimes. Then one morning she heard commotion outside. The people of Jericho were scrambling. They were confused and scared. Think about living in Jericho and watching the Israelites march around your city one time every day for six days. Then on the seventh day, the Israelites did something different. After they marched around the city, they did it again. Over and over. Everyone inside the city was afraid.

The tension was mounting. And then, the shout. I have never experienced an earthquake, but that's how I imagine it felt. I don't believe it was a slow rumble and fall. Scripture says the wall fell down flat. Those inside had no time to react. Joshua sent the same spies to rescue Rahab and her family.

Rahab needed faith that the spies would honor their word. Otherwise, she and her family would die with the rest of the city. What made the difference in her ability to trust the spies to keep their word was her faith in their God. Rahab and her family joined the Israelites, and she married a man named Salmon. They had a son named Boaz who later married Ruth, the great grandmother of David. Rahab was honored to be named in the lineage of Jesus.

My Diamond Rock of Faith

A diamond is the strongest of the precious stones. As we delve into the many jewels in our spiritual jewelry box, the diamond is first because it represents the best of all the treasures. Our faith includes strength, love, peace, and hope. These are wrapped up in our faith and in the representation of a diamond. I want people to look at my life and say, "Look at her rock," referring to the Rock of my Salvation, not a ring on my finger. Experience dictates that a ring on my finger as a symbol of love can change; however, a diamond of faith reflecting Christ in my heart never changes. I want my faith in Christ to be reflected in how I live based on His words. I want others to want what I have, so I can share Christ with them.

Our rock, Christ, as revealed through the Word of God, is expensive. It costs something. It cost Christ His life, and it costs us our time and effort. Our faith results in actions reflecting our beliefs. When disappointments come, our faith to persevere is heightened by our beliefs in action stemming from that faith.

What about you? How's that spiritual jewelry box looking?

Treasure Hunt

Stop and think about your faith. List three facets of your faith: three things from Scripture that define who you are. Don't just say, "I believe it all." Pick three. Do these things represent how you live and your obedience to God?

Spend some time in God's Word thinking about your faith. Pick a faith scripture to place in your spiritual jewelry box.

Here are three scriptures referencing our Rock.

"When my heart is overwhelmed; Lead me to
the rock that is higher than I" (Psalm 61:2).

"He only is my rock and my salvation; He is my defense;
I shall not be greatly moved" (Psalm 62:2).

"In God is my salvation and my glory; The rock of my strength,
and my refuge, is in God" (Psalm 62:7).

7

A Girl's Best Friend

"I will never leave you or forsake you" (Hebrews 13:5).

When my daughter was eleven, she heard about an internet site where you could connect with friends from high school. She thought this was a cool idea and encouraged me to join. She helped me find it and set up my profile to locate old classmates. It was kind of fun. A few years later I received an email through this classmate site from a guy I went to church with during junior high and high school. We didn't attend the same school, but because he knew which high school I attended, he was able to find me. He was divorced and was thinking about me and wondered what I was doing. He later said he assumed I was probably happily married with a two-story house, white picket fence, two cars, two dogs, and the obligatory 2.5 children. Little did he know I had been through my second devastating divorce from my children's father. That guy became a rekindled friendship who later became my wonderful husband and new best friend.

Social Media Friends

You may think I'm going to trash this avenue of friendship and its lack of reality, but I love some of these sites. Social media has made it possible for me to reconnect with friends I lost touch with over the years. I found a friend from elementary school that I hadn't spoken to in many, many years. She was a good childhood friend even though she might not have realized the impact she had on my life. I was privileged to reconnect with her across the miles and be able to pray for her when she lost her mom. Though I couldn't be with her, I could intercede on her behalf personally because of the information provided through this means of social media friendship.

I'm still looking for a good friend from high school. She moved to our school her junior year. It was hard for her because she left her friends of years behind. I heard that she shook the dust off her feet regarding our high school when she left for college because the transition was difficult and kids were mean. But she was a good friend to me, and I would love to meet up with her again.

I found a friend from 6th grade who now lives in New Zealand. Social media has allowed me to reacquaint myself with old friends and keep up with their lives through postings and pictures. If I happen to run into an old friend or see someone I haven't seen in a while, we automatically have common ground due to keeping up with each other through these venues even though we haven't interacted personally in years.

A couple of years ago I enjoyed a high school reunion where I felt like I knew many classmates better now than I did then, all because of social media.

My church youth group was unusually close and has been able to reconnect and keep up with each other's families and aging parents this way. We have planned get togethers, attended funerals, and provided prayer support for each other due to a reconnection via this media. I have renewed friendships and been able to share in other's past experiences that have both strengthened my faith and rejuvenated my prayer life.

One of my best friends moved away, but through this venue and email, we can stay in touch with our own timeframes, time zones, and schedules. The internet fills in the gaps between phones calls.

A good friend from early adult years moved away many years ago and we lost touch. We have reconnected through social media, and I hope one day to see her again in person if we are ever in her part of the country.

I have also developed an accountability relationship with a friend I met at a writer's conference who lives in another state. This wouldn't be possible, at least not as easily, if it weren't for today's technology.

While this is a great way to keep up with friends and I love it, I don't believe it captures the heart of the true meaning of the word *friend*, at least not from a biblical perspective. Let's look at a few biblical friendships and what Scripture says about friendship.

Biblical Friends

David and Jonathan were friends. They had a love for each other. Jonathan protected David when Jonathan's father, Saul, planned to kill him. Even though Jonathan had a right to the throne as the next king, he acknowledged that David would be king over Israel. He didn't allow God's blessings on David to hinder their relationship. Jonathan set aside any sense of pride or entitlement to what should have been rightfully his.

David also loved Jonathan. Many years after Jonathan's death, David sought out anyone left of the house of Saul to show kindness for Jonathan's sake (2 Samuel 9:1). Mephibosheth was a son of Jonathan who was lame in his feet. David found him and made sure he, his family, and his servants were taken care of.

Elijah and Elisha had a special friendship which involved mentorship. Some call it a holy friendship. When Elijah left Bethel, Elisha went with him. He was devoted to his older friend and mentor. Their friendship was one of encouragement, support, and leadership.

At any point in our lives, we should also be involved in developing friends through mentorship. In the book of Acts, Barnabas, Paul, and Timothy are an example of this. We should have a Paul in our lives that we are learning from and a Timothy in our lives that we are pouring into. We should also have a Barnabas as a friend that stands beside us with whom we provide mutual encouragement. These become holy friendships as portrayed by Elijah and Elisha.

God says in Scripture that Abraham was His friend (Isaiah 41:8). He was called the friend of God because of His faith, believing God (James 2:23).

God spoke to Moses face to face, as a man speaks to his friend (Exodus 33:11).

Jesus called the disciples His friends in John 15 as He shared with them all from the Father. The disciples were His closest group of friends. They spent time together strengthening and sharpening one another and from there went out among the lost. They mingled with the lost not as a social engagement for fun but as an influence. Not to engage in sin but to provide a testimony.

The disciples were friends in ministry partnership. After seeing Jesus ascend to heaven, they gathered in prayer and in fellowship. Scripture says they were in one accord. They shared the same mindset and passion. Their friendship was one of support. After Peter and James were released from prison for speaking in the name of Jesus, they went back to their friends and prayer warriors.

Throughout the book of Acts as the church started and began to grow, there are several references to friendships. Paul and Barnabas were friends. Paul and Silas were friends. Paul and Timothy were friends. The great work that Paul did was supported by the friends he had and their prayers for him and his ministry.

We also have biblical advice about friends and the character of true friendship. Choose friends carefully. Friends love each other. To have friends we must be a friend. Friends hold us accountable and give life-giving counsel. Friends support each other. Friends rejoice together, sorrow together, and share life together.

What is a Friend?

A friend is generally defined as a person you know, like, and trust; maybe an acquaintance or a supporter; or one that is not hostile. There is quite a difference between someone you like and trust and someone not hostile. Merriam Webster has a dictionary for English language learners that defines a friend as a person you like or enjoy being with.[1] That's the simplest, most straightforward definition. But is that what a true friend is?

We use the word *friendship* loosely. Friends can mean acquaintances or best friends. We have business acquaintances, work friends, church friends, neighbors, service providers (hair stylist, spa, coffee shop, doctor, nurse, dentist), friends of friends, and conference acquaintances. It's hard to know what someone actually means when they refer to a friend. Social media is a great example. Some people may have 100 friends and others 1,200 friends. A pastor of a large church may have more friends because everyone in his church has sent him a friend request. In today's culture, a friend might be better defined as someone you have met or had some type of positive influence or experience with.

I believe the real definition of a friend is better summed up in what we would call a true friend or a best friend. What is a best friend? If a friend is someone you like or enjoy being with, it stands to reason that a best friend is someone you like most and enjoy being with more than others.

Would you agree that a best friend is someone that shares what's going on in your life or someone that knows your secrets? There are no secrets between best friends. A best friend is someone that's there for you in good times and bad. They know everything about you. You share the same friends and enemies. A best friend listens. A best friend forgives. A best friend holds you accountable and brings out the best in you.

I read one definition of a best friend as the first person you think of when making plans. I like that one.

I researched the best qualities of a friend from the internet, articles, and my own social media research. While men tended to give one-word answers versus more lengthy answers from women, they both said the same thing. I gathered more than fifty different qualities. I've grouped and narrowed this list to seven. Characteristics of a friend are someone faithful, trustworthy, who shows unconditional love, who listens, who forgives, who is honest, and who is available. A best friend is a benefit to us. They meet our needs. A true best friend can be summed up in someone we want to do the same for.

Diamonds and Dogs

I have heard all my life that diamonds are a girl's best friend. When a guy walks out on you, always keep the diamond. Diamonds don't cheat, they don't lie, they don't forget, and they don't leave. They add bling to your life. They always sparkle and are never dull and boring. Diamonds light up a room. Diamonds represent love, truth, and beauty. The diamond is one of four gems labeled as precious stones and is considered to be the hardest mineral on earth. Maybe that's why we refer to diamonds as rocks.

What makes a diamond a girl's best friend? According to the song by the same name, diamonds are reliable. They don't grow cold or lose their shape or lose their charm. When others disappoint, diamonds are a girl's best friend.

We have also heard that a dog is man's best friend. Let's compare both to the seven characteristics identified above.

What are the main characteristics of a diamond and a dog in relation to a best friend?

Contrary to the song, a diamond offers nothing of true value in the way of friendship. It might be considered trustworthy and faithful in its physical quality of strength, but it offers no love, forgiveness, ears to listen, and honest feedback. And it is only available if you remember to make it available. There is no life to this friendship.

A dog is faithful, loyal, and offers unconditional love. You may have heard the story about the test of true friendship. If a man places his wife and his dog in the trunk, who is happy to see him when he opens the trunk? The dog, of course; but that isn't necessarily friendship. It's a lack of the ability to reason. But sometimes I wonder if our ability to reason gets in the way of our friendships. We harbor animosity and reason out things in our minds that might not be true. I'm not saying I support a man locking his wife, or dog, in the trunk, but the contrast is that for humans, friendship is a choice.

The following is a eulogy of a dog offered by George Vest, an attorney in 1870, representing a man whose dog had been killed by another.

> The best friend a man has in the world may turn against him and become his enemy. His son or daughter whom he has reared with loving care may prove ungrateful. Those who are nearest and dearest to us, those whom we trust with our happiness and our good name, may become traitors to their faith. The money that a man has he may lose. It flies away from him perhaps when he needs it most. A man's reputa-

tion may be sacrificed in a moment of ill-considered action. The people who are prone to fall on their knees to do us honor when success is with us may be the first to throw the stone of malice when failure settles its cloud upon our heads. The one absolutely unselfish friend that a man can have in this selfish world, the one that never deserts him, the one that never proves ungrateful or treacherous, is the dog. Gentlemen of the jury, a man's dog stands by him in prosperity and in poverty, in health and in sickness. He will sleep on the cold ground when the wintry winds blow and the snow drives fiercely, if only he can be near his master's side. He will kiss the hand that has no food to offer, he will lick the wounds and sores that come in encounter with the roughness of the world. He guards the sleep of his pauper master as if he were a prince. When all other friends desert, he remains. When riches take wings and reputation falls to pieces, he is as constant in his love as the sun in its journey through the heavens. If fortune drives the master forth an outcast into the world, friendless and homeless, the faithful dog asks no higher privilege than that of accompanying him, to guard him against danger, to fight against his enemies. And when the last scene of all comes, and death takes his master in its embrace and his body is laid in the cold ground, no matter if all other friends pursue their way, there by his graveside will the noble dog be found, his head between his paws and his eyes sad but open, in alert watchfulness, faithful and true, even unto death.[2]

What a great tribute to our canine friends. But one major thing remains. There is no option to this friendship. A dog is a dog without much reasoning or choice. While a dog may seem faithful, he doesn't understand your sorrow, can't speak words of truth to you, and doesn't hold you accountable. We all need a best friend that will never fail.

The Best Friend

Even our absolute best friends sometimes fail. That is why forgiveness was listed. Mr. Wonderful is my best friend, but he isn't perfect. There is only one who can be a true best friend, and His name is Jesus. The Bible lists nine attributes that we all want in a friend called the fruit of the Spirit. The fruit of the Spirit is love, joy, peace, patience, kindness, goodness, faithfulness, gentleness, and self-control (from Galatians 5:22-23). It's amazing how our deepest desires for a friend are met in Scripture pointing to our ultimate best friend.

Look again at each of the characteristics people indicated they wanted in a friend in my research:

Faithful

Trustworthy

Unconditional love

Listens

Forgives

Honesty

Availability

There is only one friend that meets and exceeds them all. And only in that friendship are we blessed with the true attributes of the fruit of the Spirit.

The Diamond Friendship

Throughout my first marriage and divorce, I didn't have any close friends. The people at work were the closest I had as my support group. God was my best, closest, and only true friend. As a pastor's wife, you can't share with anyone when your marriage is falling apart and their pastor is not who they think he is or expect him to be. Now my marriage is based on God as my best friend first and then my husband.

Only one diamond represents true and lasting friendship. It is greater than all. It's the diamond that heals wounds, loves the lost soul, and brings beauty to the wearer. This diamond is the One providing friendship better than any you have had. This diamond never leaves you, gossips, denies, cheats, or hurts.

This diamond gives perfect love, and it never fails. It is this girl's best friend. Unlike other friendships, my best friend can also be best friends with others and still provide everything I need from our relationship.

The classic song says diamonds are a girl's best friend, but I remember singing a different song as a child that said, "My best friend is Jesus." He is my best friend and can also be yours.

If Jesus is our best friend, then wouldn't we share the same friends and enemies? James 4:4 says, "friendship with the world is enmity with God" and "whoever wishes to be a friend of the world makes himself an enemy of God."

If Jesus is our best friend, then He would share what He knows with me, and I would share with Him. In John 15:12-15 Jesus talks about friends. Verse 15 says, ". . . I have called you friends, for all that I have heard from my Father I have made known to you." I love how all He heard from the Father, He made known to us. These words are free and readily available. They are the diamonds of our friendship with Jesus. They are the precious stones in His Word. He is speaking, but you can't hear if you're not there. He has shared with us. Are we sharing with Him?

Talk to Jesus today, and place the diamonds of a true best friend inside your jewelry box. This diamond is the most dazzling, brilliant diamond of all because it is spotless and completely pure, without a single defect.

What do your social media friend lists look like? Who are your best friends? Do they represent the world? You don't have to get rid of them, but you may need to let Jesus be your best friend first so that you can then be their best friend through the fruit of the Spirit you receive through your friendship with Christ.

In relation to these seven characteristics, what kind of friend are we to God? Is His friendship with us a two-way friendship? Jesus is our best friend, but are we like Abraham? Can He refer to us as His friend? Are you a friend of God? In John 15:15, Jesus calls us friends. In John 15:16, He says, "You did not choose Me, but I chose you and appointed you that you should go and bear fruit." He chose us as friends. We need to uphold our side of the friendship.

Treasure Hunt

Stop and think about your best friend. List five qualities of this friendship. Does your friend ever fail you in any of these areas? What about Jesus? Think about how you can remember that He is your real best friend. His love never fails.

Choose a faith scripture to place in your spiritual jewelry box that reminds you of His qualities as your friend. I suggest reading through John 15:9-17.

Sapphires of Strength

Introduction

How did I get to this place? Standing in my backyard, locked out of my house, a crowbar in my hands. It's not normal to break into your own house. My brother-in-law looked at me with a mix of uncertainty. He couldn't shatter the window for me. I had to do it. It was my house. The legal authority was mine alone.

I pulled the crowbar back and swung it like a bat. The sound of glass shattering echoed in the wind. I reached in and unlocked what was left of the window. I carefully climbed inside, unlocked the back door for my brother-in-law, and let him in the house.

The day before had seen another fight in my unhappy home. I left and went to my sister's house for the night. When I came home the next morning to collect some things, the locks had been changed on all the doors. Thus, the crowbar and resulting break-in.

I collected some clothes and went to the bathroom where I kept my jewelry. It was all gone, nowhere to be found. Just another unusual piece to the puzzle of my first marriage that didn't seem to fit. Nothing made sense. As I look back today, much of it still doesn't. I'll never know what my ex-husband's purpose was in taking my jewelry, especially since the locks on the house had been changed.

I asked myself what I was doing without really expecting an answer. I didn't feel any authority over my life. I didn't have any answers, just exhaustion. My fragile heart shattered just like my back window by a crowbar of fear, exhaustion, and uncertainty.

Survival came through the authority of God's Word piecing my heart back together and exchanging my weakness for His strength. Whatever you are going through or have been through, God gives strength.

8

The Tablet of Your Heart

"My soul melts from heaviness; Strengthen me according to Your word" (Psalm 119:28).

Who controls the TV remote at your house? While I may not control the TV remote, I am a bit of a control freak and like things done my way in other areas. Mr. Wonderful says I'm OCD because I like to organize things in a certain way. I can tell if someone moves something I organized, and it needs to move back. It's part of my controlling nature. I've discovered what OCD stands for in my life.

OCD = Overcoming Crises Daily

That's right. Someone with what my husband terms in me as OCD must overcome crises daily that others don't worry about.

For example:

- The toilet paper must roll in the correct direction. Have you ever found yourself in a public restroom changing the roll of toilet paper to the correct direction? I confess that I've done this.

- Silverware place settings must be correct. The fork belongs on the left, the knife is on the right with the blade facing toward the plate. Have you ever rearranged the silverware at a restaurant, or worse, at a friend's house when invited for dinner? I'm not confessing anything here.

There are other daily crises I experience.

- The stress in a drive-through line where the person in front of you doesn't pull up far enough for you to place your order. I experience crisis when the voice from the speaker asks for my order, and I'm not quite close enough for them to hear me without shouting. People two blocks away can hear my order, but the voice on the other end of the speaker can't. Just pull up already.

- A bank balance off more than $10 or $1 or, okay, even a penny. Such is my crisis.

- Spices not returned to the pantry in alphabetical order (yes, I am serious). This becomes a crisis when making the grocery list and then purchasing items that are in the wrong place. I may or may not have five tins of pepper because someone that shall remain nameless moved the pepper.

- A microwave showing seconds left on the display after heating food. This happens at my office when someone is heating up their lunch and removes it before the time is up. Why don't they clear the seconds remaining? I don't understand how they can just leave it and others can walk by and not notice. More than once I have looked at the time and wondered how it was already after 1:00 pm only to realize that was the remaining cooking time and not the clock time. Crisis.

- Scripture quoted in a different version than what you learned as a child. Don't people know certain verses have to be quoted in King James? John 3:16: "For God so loved the world that He gave His only begotten Son that who-so-ever believ-eth in Him should not perish but have everlasting life." None of this "one and only," it's "only begotten." And it's e-v-e-r-l-a-s-t-i-n-g life.

Speaking of Scripture, it surprises Mr. Wonderful that I haven't purchased a Bible where the books are in alphabetical order. Do they make those? The Old Testament would be Amos to Zephaniah (it's not chronological anyway). The New Testament would be Acts to Titus, and John would be the first gospel book instead of the last. This makes sense because churches always tell new Christians to begin reading the Gospel of John when Matthew is first.

Do you have any OCD tendencies? Or maybe you deal with daily crises of a different nature. Are you lonely, fighting depression, dealing with aging parents or teens that think they should be the parents? Do you need healing, do you have financial challenges, do you need a job? Does the state of morality, or lack thereof, in our country weigh heavily on you? What eats you up inside when you lose control? What controls you? What have you let become an obsession? Enough questions.

1 Corinthians 6:12 says, "All things are lawful for me, but all things are not helpful. All things are lawful for me, but I will not be brought under the power of any."

What a powerful phrase – brought under the power. Some versions say enslaved, mastered, dominated, but I like the NKJV that says "brought under the power," which is exactly what it means. I don't want to be brought under the power or controlled by anything other than God's Word.

In his books *#struggles,* Craig Groeschel asks several questions.

"Is checking your phone the last thing you do every day?

"What about when you wake up? Is checking your phone one of the first things you do every morning?

"Do you feel compelled to check your phone while waiting in line at the fast-food drive through, in the checkout lane at the store, or while waiting in the airport? More than once?"[1]

He then states the following in reference to 1 Corinthians 6:12.

"The power of Christ in me should be stronger than anything else in my life. I will not be mastered by an addiction to food. I will not be mastered by material possessions … I will not be mastered by what other people think of me."[2]

Who or what controls you? What brings you under its power? What zaps your strength? In a world overrun with things that we want to control or that want to control us, we need an unfailing and unbreakable source of strength. Maybe that's why God wrote His first prescription for strength on a tablet of sapphire.

Sapphires

Sapphires are known for strength. The Ten Commandments were written on a tablet of precious stone that many scholars believe to have been sapphire.

I used to picture the tablets of stone in Moses' hands as something similar to clay. I thought they must have broken and crumbled easily when he dropped them. But if they were in fact made of sapphire, the breaking was a bigger deal than I originally assumed. I went back and studied these passages again to see what I might have missed about these stones that were so precious, not only because of their strength but because of the words of God on them.

Exodus 24:9-12 "... under His feet as it were a paved work of sapphire stones ... tablets of stone."

Exodus 31:18 "And when He had made an end of speaking with him on Mount Sinai, He gave Moses two tablets of the Testimony, tablets of stone, written with the finger of God."

Exodus 32:16 "Now the tablets were the work of God, and the writing was the writing of God engraved on the tablets."

Exodus 32:19 "... he cast the tablets out of his hands and broke them at the foot of the mountain."

Deuteronomy 5:22 "... He wrote them on two tablets of stone and gave them to me."

Deuteronomy 9:10 "Then the Lord delivered to me two tablets of stone written with the finger of God, and on them were all the words which the Lord had spoken to you . . ."

Matthew Erwin, in an article from his website, appleeye. org, discusses a teaching of rabbinical Judaism as found in the Talmud and Mishnah that the tablets of the law were made of sapphire.[3] When Moses and the elders of Israel go up the mountain, Exodus 24:10 references a paved work of sapphire stone under God's feet. Then Moses is commanded to go up farther on the mountain where God gave him tablets of stone with His commandments. Erwin states, "The stone from which the tablets were fashioned almost certainly refers to that which appeared to be sapphire only two verses earlier. The sapphire is the only type of stone mentioned in the context." Exodus 32:16 states "the tablets were the work of God, and the writing was the writing of God engraved on the tablets." Some believe that the tablets were not only sapphire stone but were carved from God's throne based on the correlation between Exodus 24:10 and 12.

In *The Legends of the Jews* (Volume 3) by Louis Ginzberg, "Moses departed from the heavens with the two tables on which the Ten Commandments were engraved, and just the words of it are by nature Divine, so too are the tables on which they are engraved. These were created by God's own hand in the dusk of the first Sabbath at the close of the creation and were made of a sapphire-like stone."[4]

Referring to the stones in the breastplate of Aaron, Ginzberg states, "Issachar's stone was the sapphire, for this tribe devoted themselves completely to the study of the Torah, and it is this very stone, the sapphire, out of which the two tables of the law were hewn."[5]

Isaiah 54:11 references a foundation of sapphire and in Revelation 21:19 sapphire is listed as the second foundation of wall of the New Jerusalem.

The skeptic that I am questioned how easily a stone as strong as sapphire could break. I discovered that while sapphire is strong and scratch resistant, it is subject to cracks and can shatter if hit sharply. So perhaps God used tablets made with the strength of a precious stone of sapphire to record His words to the children of Israel through Moses. What I do know is that today He writes on the tablet of our hearts.

"You are our epistle written in our hearts,
known and read by all men; clearly you are an epistle of Christ,
ministered by us, written not with ink but by the Spirit
of the living God, not on tablets of stone but on tablets of flesh,
that is, of the heart" (2 Corinthians 3:2-3).

"Keep my words, and treasure my commands within you. Bind
them on your fingers; Write them on the tablet of your heart"
(Proverbs 7:1,3).

Placing His words on the tablet of our heart makes us strong like the stone of sapphire. It is scratch resistant, but as we all know from experiences in our lives, sometimes our hearts are shattered. It's in these times that God can again give us the words we need to transform those experiences into treasured truths if we allow Him to comfort and strengthen us.

Tablets

When I hear the word tablet, different things come to mind. The doctor prescribes tablets to cure aches and pains. When I started first grade, I wrote on a Big Chief tablet with wide spaced lines using a thick pencil to learn to make letters and numbers correctly. Many years earlier, children wrote on slate tablets. Today we have electronic tablets to write on using a keyboard or by dragging our finger across the screen.

We write every day. We write lists to remember things. I make grocery lists, to-do lists, errand lists, home organization lists, and cleaning lists. I use a bullet journal where I set up my preferred calendar systems and track my habits, goals, and accomplishments. My life is recorded within a combination of my bullet journal and an on-line spreadsheet. Today I am writing this book on an electronic tablet.

The word write is a verb. It means to mark, inscribe, or engrave on something. God wrote to us through those He instructed so His words would be remembered. God told Moses to write about the victory over the Amalekites. Moses wrote the words of the Lord. God told Isaiah to write for future generations. God told Habakkuk to write the vision he was given. And Jeremiah 31:33 says God would write in the hearts of His children.

Proverbs tells us to write mercy and truth on the tablet of our hearts. We are to write God's words on the tablet of our heart. We write so we will remember, and so others will know and remember too. Isaiah 49:16 says that God has engraved us on the palms of His hands. When God writes on the tablet of our heart, He engraves Himself onto our soul.

A tablet also represents forgiveness. Our sin is etched into the tablet of our heart so deep that we can't remove it. In Jeremiah 17:1 God speaks of Judah's sin and says, "With the point of a diamond it is engraved on the tablet of their heart." But God has the ultimate eraser. His eraser doesn't just erase the surface. It cleans out the porous areas that have absorbed our sin. He wipes our slate clean down to the deepest crevice. Jeremiah prays for deliverance, and in chapter 18 God compares us to a vessel of clay marred in the hand of the potter, "so he made it again into another vessel, as it seemed good to the potter to make." Then He says, "Look, as the clay is in the potter's hand, so are you in My hand." He re-forms us and makes us new.

In Exodus 34:1 God told Moses that He would write on the tablets. God wrote the Ten Commandments on a tablet of stone with His finger. I guess tablets of stone were to God what electronic tablets are to us today.

There is an App for That

We also have applications on today's tablets. We have apps for everything from maps to music to books to church services to social interactions. If you can think of it, somebody has or is working on an app for it. Pull out your phone or your tablet. What apps do you have there? The apps on our electronic devices sometimes reflect the apps on our heart. They can strengthen us or make us weak. Compare these apps to the apps on the tablet of your heart. What's on your app, or do you even have this app downloaded in your heart?

Camera and Gallery – Reflections of what we look at and capture in our minds.

Books/Music – What we read and listen to.

Calendar – How we spend our time.

Fitness – Staying spiritually fit.

Social Media – Do we communicate with God as much as others?

Games – Are we playing games with life? Are addictions keeping us from hearing God's voice?

Settings – Is it time to rest or default to the basics?

1 Corinthians 1:25 "Because the foolishness of God is wiser than men, and the weakness of God is stronger than men."

One of my verses for strength in my spiritual jewelry box is Psalm 119:28, "My soul melts from heaviness; Strengthen me according to Your word." When I hear or read the word *melting*, I think of ice cream melting in the heat of the day or snow melting beneath the sun's rays. The word can mean to pour out or weep. When burdens, grief, or stresses increase, my soul begins to melt. I pour out my struggles to God and sometimes weep with their weight.

The psalmist asks God to strengthen him. This implies rising up, standing up, and being established. But he doesn't ask God just to give the strength, but to give it according to God's Word. The strength we need comes from His words to us. That is why His words must be hidden in the spiritual jewelry box of our heart. God promises they will not return void. There in our heart we turn to God through His words for the strength to rise again and move forward in life for His glory.

What's the main app for the tablet of our hearts? It's our spiritual jewelry box. But the app is empty if we haven't filled it. Download God's treasured truths into your spiritual jewelry box, and let God write on the tablet of your heart.

Tamar's Strength

Scripture tells us Tamar was married to Judah's oldest son, Er, who was wicked and died. Judah told his next son, Onan, to marry Tamar and give her children as an heir to his brother Er, as was customary during that time. But Onan died also. So Judah told Tamar to remain a widow in her father's house until his youngest son, Shelah, was grown. She waited those years as asked. Shelah grew up, yet she was ignored or forgotten. The custom and morals during that time required Judah's family to provide her with a husband so she would not die a childless widow, either by one of his sons or even himself.

During this time Judah's wife also died. When Judah was traveling away from home, Tamar dressed as a harlot, covered her face, and met him on the road. Judah was in mourning for his wife and slept with Tamar, supposing her to be a harlot. He offered her a goat as payment, but she asked for a pledge until the goat would be sent. He gave her his signet and cord and his staff. When Judah sent the goat to her as payment via his friend, no one could find this woman. Three months later word came to Judah that Tamar had been unfaithful and was pregnant. Judah commanded she be killed. She then sent word to him that by the man to whom the signet, cord, and staff belonged she was pregnant. Judah knew they were his and said, "She has been more righteous than I, because I did not give her to Shelah my son."[6]

Tamar was left alone when her husband died and then her next husband died and then Judah promised her his third son, yet never made good on his word. She took matters into her own hands to have children. She was left alone in weakness once again when Judah ordered her to be killed. Right or wrong, Judah said she was more righteous than he. She gave birth to twins, one named Perez. Her strength resulted in the offspring in the lineage of Jesus. A strength she claimed like sapphire drawn from the promises of God's words.

In what area of life are you weak? God's words to us provide the strength we need to move forward. They provide the catalyst to exchange our weakness for His strength. Tamar stood strong in what she believed was right, which led to eternal dividends for all of us. God can do the same for us through His words etched on those original sapphire tablets and throughout all the scriptures we have available to us today, resulting in future dividends we may not see now but can rest assured will be there.

Treasure Hunt

Look up 2 Corinthians 1:8-10. To be burdened beyond measure is a burden above strength, but God delivers. What other treasures do you find here? Place these treasures in your spiritual jewelry box.

9

The Great Exchange

"My grace is sufficient for you, for My strength is made perfect in weakness" (2 Corinthians 12:9).

Our back yard is sparse as far as landscaping goes. We have two fig trees which have grown over the years but not much else. Not long ago, Mr. Wonderful planted a small vegetable garden. About two weeks later, torrential rains descended. The ground couldn't dry out before another round of storms came in, bringing heavy downpours of rain, gusting winds, and threats of hail. We worried about the small plants in the garden. Would they be beaten down by the hail? Would the winds and rain uproot or drown them? But never once did we worry about the fig trees. They were strong and deeply rooted in the ground. The gusty winds made the branches bend back and forth, and they lost a few leaves. But they stood strong. We had good reason not to worry.

This reminds me of how we survive the storms of life. Are we more likely to be beaten down, uprooted, or drowned? Jesus gave an example of two types of homes during a storm. One was built on a rock foundation and stood firm when the storms came. The other was built on the sand and washed away. The contrast represents the difference in our lives when we are obedient to His words. It all starts with knowing His words. It's what we are rooted and grounded in that makes the difference. When tough times come, our strength is determined by where we are planted.

The Strength of a Tree

I love the imagery in Psalm 1:3 of the man who delights in and meditates on God's Word. The psalmist says he will be like a tree planted by the rivers of water bringing forth fruit in its season.

"Blessed is the man who walks not in the counsel of the ungodly, Nor stands in the path of sinners, nor sits in the seat of the scornful; but his delight is in the law of the Lord, and in His law he meditates day and night. He shall be like a tree planted by the rivers of water, that brings forth its fruit in its season, whose leaf also shall not wither; and whatever he does shall prosper" (Psalm 1:1-3).

Scripture repeats the same imagery, although more in-depth, in Jeremiah 17. Jeremiah contrasts the man who trusts in his own strength versus trusting in God.

"Thus says the Lord: "Cursed is the man who trusts in man and makes flesh his strength, whose heart departs from the Lord. For he shall be like a shrub in the desert, and shall not

see when good comes, but shall inhabit the parched places in
the wilderness, in a salt land which is not inhabited"
(verses 5-6).

"Blessed is the man who trusts in the Lord, and whose hope
is the Lord. For he shall be like a tree planted by the waters,
which spreads out its roots by the river, and will not fear when
heat comes; but its leaf will be green, and will not be anxious
in the year of drought, nor will cease from yielding fruit"
(verses 7-8).

Scripture does not say what kind of tree, but I picture a strong tree impenetrable by winds or storms. In north central Texas, Bradford pears are a popular tree in neighborhoods, especially new developments. These are fruitless trees that grow quickly and are beautiful and lush. The problem with the Bradford pear is that it is a weak tree. When storms come through with strong winds, these trees are more likely to have branches broken off or to split down the middle. Many homeowners end up having to remove the broken tree and plant another. We currently have one Bradford pear in our front yard. While the two homes across from us have had theirs removed due to storm damage, ours is still standing. This is due in part to the location of the tree and in part to our consistent pruning of the tree to help it remain strong. Still, we know there is the possibility our tree may one day also become a north Texas storm casualty and need to be removed.

The tree depicted in Psalm 1 and Jeremiah 17 is not a tree you would need to be concerned about. It is strong like an oak and large like a California redwood. I remember visiting redwood forests in California several times as a child. There was a tree you could drive through and a tree said to have housed several people during a storm through a hollowed area in its trunk. You can walk inside this tree and marvel at its size. There is no known insect that can destroy a redwood tree. Fire is not a big threat because the trunk is thick with a lot of water inside, and the bark doesn't have flammable resin like a pine tree does.[1]

I picture the tree in this passage planted next to a cool, clear stream with water rushing from a waterfall a few miles away. Its roots stretch out along the banks of the stream. It has large luscious green leaves. And the branches bear large, juicy fruit of all kinds.

There is a sharp contrast here in Jeremiah. You've probably had to make decisions before where you listed the pros and cons of a choice. You contrast the good and bad. Let's do that here. There are five differences between the one who trusts in man and the one who trusts in the Lord.

- Those who trust in man make flesh their strength, and their hearts turn away from God. Jesus quotes Isaiah saying they serve God with their mouth but not their heart.[2] Jesus spoke about the Pharisees being more concerned about the outside than the inside. They made a great show of observing traditions and rituals to please men, but God looks for what is in the heart. 1 Samuel 16:7 states, "Man looks at the outward appearance, but the Lord looks at the heart."

- They are compared to a shrub in the desert. Small, bare, sparse. A west Texas tumbleweed comes to mind.

- They shall not see any good come to them. Have you ever known someone who didn't see good in anything?

Someone always negative. Trusting in yourself causes that. At best their cup is only half full, but usually it's half empty. They are stagnant. Reminds me of the Dead Sea.

• They dwell in parched places of wilderness. There are cracks in the ground. They thirst. I imagine having sand in your throat that can't be removed.

• They are in an uninhabited salt land. Alone. Desolate and barren.

The contrast:

• Those who trust in the Lord and hope in the Lord have a state of confidence and security. They are not anxious.

• They are compared to a tree planted by water as described in Psalm 1. The water needed for survival is always there. This tree doesn't have to wait for the rains to come to it. Even if the rains come farther away, they make their way to the river where the tree finds nourishment.

• They send out roots by the stream and do not fear when heat comes. There is no fear because the fresh supply of water enables the roots to stretch out and go deep enough to reach not only the water in the stream but far down within the earth. They are filled. Full of life.

• Their leaves remain green. A healthy plant has green leaves appearing polished. I have several houseplants. I don't have a green thumb, but I know when I forget to water the plants. Their leaves begin to turn yellow and then brown. The leaves are dying. I can usually refresh the plant with water, but those yellow and brown leaves die and fall off. This tree has leaves that remain green.

• They continue to bear fruit. We have all heard about drought conditions that cause fruit crops to fail. This tree continues to bear fruit.

These descriptions depict a great difference in this brittle shrub versus luscious tree. And it is all determined by who we trust. I have felt like a brittle shrub, dried up and without hope. When others beat me down and I felt worthless, I felt like a dying shrub. But unlike a tumbleweed lost in the desert, the words from Jeremiah showed me I didn't have to stay there. I could change based on who I trusted. Trusting God allowed me to tap into and gain strength from the streams of life in His Word. I was refreshed and filled. Fresh life was restored.

Cry Out for Strength

In exchanging our weakness for His strength, Psalm 107 gives four examples of God's deliverance of His people from the circumstances in their lives. In the commentary by A. R. Fausset in the Blue Letter Bible, he says in reference to Psalm 107, "Although the general theme of this Psalm may have been suggested by God's special favor to the Israelites in their restoration from captivity, it must be regarded as an instructive celebration of God's praise for His merciful providence to all men in their various emergencies."[3]

Relating this Psalm to our disappointments, God steps in whether circumstances result from our own choices or those of another. In each circumstance listed in this Psalm, it says, "Then." "Then they cried out to the Lord in their trouble," and He delivered. We need to cry out to the Lord. Then, He will deliver.

The first example in verses 4 and 5 talks about a people God had redeemed from the hand of the enemy. "They wandered in the wilderness . . . They found no city to dwell in. Hungry *(strength failing)* and thirsty, their soul fainted in them." They grew weak.

THEN. "Then they cried out to the Lord in their trouble" (verse 6).

We wander in the wilderness of disappointments. After my divorce, I wandered in my walk until I cried out to the Lord and accepted His strength. We need to cry out to the Lord in our wandering. "He delivered *(rescued)* them out of their distresses and He led them forth by the right way" (verse 6-7). He satisfied and filled them with goodness. Their weakness was replaced with His strength. In the same way, He delivers us when we are wandering. He leads us in the right way.

The second example tells of those who were "bound *(prisoners)* in affliction and irons because they rebelled against the words of God" (verses 10-11).

THEN. "Then they cried out to the Lord in their trouble" (verse 13).

There are different kinds of rebellion. While I wouldn't say I rebelled against God, there were times I questioned Him and how He could let this happen to me. I felt trapped in a prison. We need to cry out to the Lord in our rebellion whether it comes from our own disobedience or lack of faith in our time of weakness. "He saved them out of their distresses. He brought them out of darkness and the shadow of death, and broke their chains in pieces" (verses 13-14). Their prison/weakness was exchanged for His freedom/strength. He saves us from our rebellion, brings us out of darkness, and breaks the chains keeping us there.

The third example speaks of fools afflicted "because of their transgression and because of their iniquities . . . they drew near to the gates of death" (verses 17-18).

THEN. "Then they cried out to the Lord in their trouble" (verse 19).

We all sin. We need to cry out to the Lord in our sin. "He sent His word and healed them, and delivered them from their destructions" (verse 20). We trade our sin weakness for His healing. He saves us from our sin and heals us by His Word. When we know the Word, He brings it to mind. When we are searching for it and hiding it in our hearts, then He will use it to save us daily.

The fourth example talks about those doing business on great waters. God controls the waters, but "Their soul melts *(faints)* because of trouble ... and are at their wits' end" (verses 26-27). This was the end of their wisdom as men to navigate the storms.

Their weakness - His strength. In Matthew Henry's commentary, he notes that this example is given "for all similar perils, in which those that cry out unto God have ever found him a very present help."[4]

THEN. "Then they cried out to the Lord in their trouble" (verse 28).

In our daily life, God is there, but our circumstances cause our soul to melt, and we meet our wits' end. Even in my deepest, darkest night, God stood next to me. Storms inevitably come into our lives. God can immediately calm them, or He can walk us through them and deliver us on the other side.

In Daniel 3:19-23, Shadrach, Meshach, and Abednego were thrown into a burning fiery furnace for worshipping

God instead of King Nebuchadnezzar. They were not delivered from going into the furnace. Instead, they were delivered from within and out of the furnace. Scripture shows God was with them as evidenced by the fourth man. Paul was not delivered from his thorn in the flesh but was given God's grace and His strength to endure.

We are not always delivered from life's disappointments, but as we cry out to the Lord in our storms of life, we are delivered from within those trials. "He calms the storm so that its waves are still ... He guides them to their desired haven" (verses 29-30). God calms the storms in our lives and guides us to safe havens whether immediate or in the midst.

If we are wandering, if we have rebelled, if we have sinned, if we are caught in the storms of life, He will deliver and save. He leads, He breaks our chains, He heals through His word, and He gives calm in the storm.

After each instance of salvation in times of trouble, the psalmist says, "Oh that men would give thanks to the Lord for His goodness, and for His wonderful works to the children of men!"

Oh that men would give thanks to the Lord. This is part of where we receive strength. We give thanks. Thank you, Lord.

God satisfies and fills our hungry soul with goodness. He breaks our prisons, our chains, gates of bronze, and bars of iron. And all He asks in return is our thanksgiving and declaration of His works with rejoicing. He requests we exalt and praise Him in the company of others.

After these four examples of trouble, deliverance, and thanksgiving, God's power is shown in the following verses. It contrasts His power to turn abundance to deprivation and deprivation to abundance.

Verse 33 "He turns rivers into a wilderness, and the watersprings into dry ground."

Contrasted with

Verse 35 "He turns a wilderness into pools of water, and dry land into watersprings."

My prayer 107:35: Lord, turn my wilderness situations into pools of water and my dry land into watersprings. Thank you. I will declare Your works. I will exalt You and praise You.

By crying out to the Lord in my distress, He exchanged my weakness for His strength.

Scaling the Heights of Fear

We are born with only two fears: the fear of falling and the fear of loud noises. Our other fears are developed. I'm afraid of heights. I don't remember when it happened. My first memory of this fear was on a Ferris wheel with my children. I was terrified "they" would fall. I thought of it more as a protection instinct than a fear, but over time it has grown worse. I get an uncontrollable physically sick feeling.

Many years ago, I visited the Statue of Liberty when you could climb a circular staircase to the top. I pressed through my fears and climbed all the way up; however, coming down proved different. Even though I couldn't see outside or how high I had climbed, I felt paralyzed. I came down the stairs by crawling backwards. There was no choice, but at times I didn't know if I would make it. The fear was real.

Could it be we miss out on mountaintop experiences with God due to our fears? In our walk with God, do we only go so far due to fear of missing the mark, or fear of falling, or fear of the valley to come?

Many times our weakness comes from fear. We can exchange our fears of the unknown, our fear of failure, and our fear of being alone for God's power, love, and a sound mind.

2 Timothy 1:7 "For God has not given us a spirit of fear, but of power and of love and of a sound mind."

In my weakness I was afraid of what was to come. Things in that first marriage were progressing from bad to worse, and I was afraid of failure. I didn't want my marriage to fail. I was afraid of being alone, yet I was never alone. God knew what was to come. Where I might fail in human pursuits, He had greater plans for me. He could take my mess and exchange it for His purpose. My weaknesses for His strength. I had to come to the point of "Then." Then I cried out to the Lord in my trouble. He exchanged my fears for His strength—His power, love, and a sound mind.

Fear can keep our roots from growing deep enough to hold us steady in the storms and to replenish our dry soul when fear makes us doubt.

Scripture says to cry out for discernment and lift up our voice for understanding. It tells us that the Lord gives wisdom, knowledge, and understanding.

Being strong is not having a hardened heart. It is not refusing to cry or suppressing the pain. A hard heart is a weakness. A hard heart is not a strong heart. Sometimes giving yourself permission to cry or grieve a loss of any kind takes more strength.

"And He said to me, "My grace is sufficient *(unfailing strength)* for you, for My strength *(power)* is made perfect *(complete)* in weakness" (2 Corinthians 12:9, parenthesis mine).

His grace is all we need. It is sufficient. The Merriam-Webster online dictionary defines sufficient as "enough to meet the needs of a situation or proposed end."[5] The online Blue Letter Bible defines the word used in this verse for sufficient as "to be possessed of unfailing strength; to be strong, to suffice, to be enough."[6] His grace and strength are enough.

Treasure Hunt

Look up Proverbs 2:3-6. What treasure do you find here?

Psalm 142. Pray this prayer from scripture and then in your own words based on your circumstances and the strength you need. Tell God where you are weak. It's okay, He already knows, but He wants you to tell Him and cry out for His strength.

Rubies of Love

Introduction

I cried every day, until one day, I didn't. The beginning of the end. I was mad, but that was the only emotion. I was hurt, yes. But no tears.

I cried so many times before. In those tears my heart seemed to crack deeper each time. I cried, but instead of melting my heart and the hurt, the tears began to freeze my heart. No longer a healing cry. It was painful. At least I felt something. But not forever. The tears began to dry around my heart, encasing it in a solid block of crustaceous salt. My own hard outer shell blocking future pain. I was better when I was just mad. Maybe I just needed to stay mad. Anger, tears, separation. The ditch was getting wider. We moved farther apart, and he didn't even know it. What was worse, he didn't care. And in the end, I didn't either.

"My flesh and my heart fail, but God is the strength of my heart and my portion forever" (Psalm 73:26). God is the strength of my heart. He alone keeps it beating. And He is all I need.

My ex-husband used to say, "I love you, but I don't like you." We want a promise from someone to love us forever, no matter what. Not possible with man alone. We like to think it is, but it's not. But you need that kind of love, you say? So do I.

An empty space exists within each of us. A longing to be wanted, needed, loved, and even liked exists in the deep recesses of our soul. Those that say they don't have this longing deceive themselves. It exists for everyone.

That space can only be filled with what it was designed for. We try to fill it with material possessions, accomplishments, education, and the love of others. But this space was not designed for man-made trophies or emotions. It was not designed for love from a parent or spouse or child. It was not designed for anything that can change or fail. It was designed for the unchanging, unfailing love of one.

"Neither death nor life, nor angels nor principalities nor powers, nor things present nor things to come, nor height nor depth, nor any other created thing, shall be able to separate us from the love of God which is in Christ Jesus our Lord"
(Romans 8:38-39).

"Jesus Christ is the same yesterday, today, and forever"
(Hebrews 13:8).

"God is love. In this the love of God was manifested toward us, that God has sent His only begotten Son into the world, that we might live through Him. In this is love, not that we loved God, but that He loved us and sent His Son to be the propitiation for our sins" (1 John 4:8-10).

"But God demonstrates His own love toward us, in that while we were still sinners, Christ died for us" (Romans 5:8).

God has a love language that permeates and fills that empty space. We need only accept and enter His circle of love. True love.

10

God's Love Language

"For God so loved the world that He gave His only
begotten Son, that whoever believes in Him should
not perish but have everlasting life" (John 3:16).

I love a good romantic comedy. Mr. Wonderful and I enjoy
watching the movie *You've Got Mail*. In a previous chapter, I
told you how Mr. Wonderful emailed me through a classmate
site. There is a little more to the story. I replied to his email,
but he never got my reply. One night I was watching this movie while my children were visiting their dad. It was always
difficult while they were gone, so a good romantic comedy to
make me laugh and let me cry was in order. During the movie, I decided to go back to that email I received weeks earlier
and be sure I had replied correctly. There it was, clear as could
be. He stated in his email that his email address had not been

updated on the site and to please reply to a different one. I did, he did, and now we are married.

This movie and other romantic stories take us to another world, a world of hope. We can feel the love, if only for a moment. And that's what we want.

I just want to be loved. It is the deepest yearning of my heart, but no one can love me like I want to be loved. I feel like the need for love makes me selfish. In this desire, I understand I must give love to others; but I don't always have the right words and don't know what to say or do. Not long ago a memory came up on social media taking me back to my own words.

If we continually and consistently place the gemstones from scripture into our hearts, we won't have to worry about what we say. The gems of God's words will overflow from our spiritual jewelry box. "For out of the abundance of the heart the mouth speaks" (Matthew 12:34).

Jesus is the only one who can love me like I want to be loved. He will always say exactly the right thing at the right moment.

Rubies

Geologists really don't know how rubies formed in the first place. That rubies even exist, says Peter Heaney, geosciences professor at Penn State University, is something of a "minor geological miracle."[1]

Rubies are a type of corundum, a rare mineral made up of densely packed aluminum and oxygen atoms, which are normally colorless. When other atoms are substituted for a few of the aluminum ones, bright hues emerge. None of this can take place, however, if silica or large amounts of iron are present. And therein lies the mystery.

Silica is one of the most abundant elements in the earth's crust, so scientists aren't sure how rubies manage to avoid silica and iron while at the same time connecting with the rare chromium. "The fluorescence [of a ruby] is tied to its composition, to the low iron. That's hard to do in geology, to get the iron that low," says (George) Harlow. "Corundum is rare enough as it is. So, adding all these things together, ruby is very rare."[2]

We can't explain rubies. We also can't explain God's love. It has always been, is all encompassing, and is never ending. It is a miracle.

Rubies of Love

I love Mr. Wonderful. He always remembers my birthday, our anniversary, and special holidays. He talks to me, and he listens to me. He wants to make me happy. We have a great relationship of knowing when something is more important to the other and knowing when to give and take. He is supportive and would gladly stand between me and harm's way. His love for me is patient, kind, sharing, hopeful, enduring, and he has promised to love me forever. Sound like the perfect guy? Sorry, he's taken. He's mine.

Despite everything good I can say about Mr. Wonderful, neither of us is perfect. And as much as he loves me, his love doesn't compare to God's love. God's love is perfect. It casts out fear. His love never fails. Even when I don't deserve it, God loves me. Even when I hurt God's feelings, He loves me. Even when I forget to talk to Him or acknowledge Him, God loves me. If I ignored Him for a year, He would still love me. Every time I sin, I mess up fellowship with God; but He loves me, and He is ready and waiting for me to turn back to Him.

God has given me rubies. He has given me every precious stone. They are like gifts all neatly wrapped and waiting to be opened. All I need to do is open them by spending time with Him in His Word. What is stopping me from filling my spiritual jewelry box? What is stopping you?

The Language of Love

The book by Gary Chapman, *The Five Love Languages*, has sold more than 8 million copies. People want to know how to communicate love to each other and to understand how they best receive love from others. In this book, he lists five basic love languages: words of affirmation, quality time, receiving gifts, acts of service, and physical touch.[3]

We also have five senses: hearing, taste, sight, smell, and touch. Many times romantically we expect to be loved through each one. We want to hear the words "I love you," taste that box of chocolates, see the bling of the diamonds, smell the roses, and feel the touch of arms around us. But these are just superficial. Gary Chapman hits the core of what he says is each person's primary love language. His book addresses expressing heartfelt commitment to your spouse. It's a great read that I recommend, but in this chapter, I want to look at the relationship between how we feel and express love in relation to God's love. I want to look at love languages in relation to how God loves us.

Your specific love language or preferred stimulus through your five senses are met by God. He doesn't use a generic one-size-fits-all love language. He speaks to each of us in our own unique and individual love language.

God's Love

All four gospels tell the miraculous story of Jesus feeding five thousand plus with only five loaves of bread and two fish. But if you go back and read what happened before this, we see that Jesus had just found out about John the Baptist's beheading. It was then Jesus decided to go to a deserted place for rest. He was grieving. He and His disciples set out for some time alone, some time with God, some time of rest. But when they arrived, a multitude had figured out where He was headed and arrived there first.

How would you feel in this situation? I would want to tell those people to leave me alone and go away. But Jesus was moved with compassion. It wasn't all about Him. It was about those that needed Him. He healed their sick and spent the afternoon teaching them. As evening came, everyone was hungry. The disciples wanted to send the people away. I'm with them. Come on, Jesus. You came here for rest, and instead you continue ministering to these people. It's time to take care of You and us. But Jesus said no and instead performed a miracle. He met not only their spiritual needs but also their physical needs. It wasn't until after their needs were met that He sent everyone away, including His disciples, so He could go up on the mountain alone and pray.

Jesus gave the people love through His words, His time, His gift, His service, and His touch. He taught them. He gave up time that He so desperately needed after hearing of His friend's death. He gave the people what they came for and more. He served and fed them miraculously. He healed their sick. You can read the entire story either in Matthew 14 or Mark 6.

He does the same for us. Whatever we need, He gives. Let's look at each one individually.

Love Through Words

God loves us through His words. I have heard the Bible called God's love letter. He provides us with history, poetry, prophecy, the gospel of salvation, and letters of encouragement. The Bible is filled with encouragement, direction, peace, love, and support. If you need a word of encouragement every day for a month, you can find it in His Word. What about for a year? Or the rest of your life? If we need affirmation, we need only look to His Word to know how much we are loved and who we are in Christ. The Holy Spirit also speaks to us in different ways depending on what we need. You can read the same passage of Scripture at different times and receive a different encouragement based on your circumstances. The words are the same, but the application can be different.

"Call to Me, and I will answer you, and show you great and mighty things, which you do not know" (Jeremiah 33:3).

Love Through Time

This one is up to us to take advantage. He is there when we are. We have God's undivided attention whenever we want it. You can be in a room with 1,000 other people praying, and God hears you individually. To the extent you make time for God, you have His time. He is with us every second. We just need to stop and make time to pray, talk to God, and spend quality time with Him.

In what way do you want someone you love to spend time with you? In the same way, God wants time with you because He loves you. Take a walk with God. Read your Bible to learn more about Him. Make a date with God. Make time every day.

> *"And you will seek Me and find Me, when you search for Me with all your heart" (Jeremiah 29:13).*

Love Through Gifts

There is no greater love and no greater gift than what God has given us through Jesus from His birth, life example, death, resurrection, and promise of eternal life. God gave us His Son. His life for ours.

We have the Holy Spirit as a comforter for living every day. Through the gift of the Holy Spirit and the gift of His Word, we receive the fruit of the Spirit (love, joy, peace, patience, kindness, goodness, faithfulness, gentleness, and self-control).

We also have God's visual symbols of love. Take a walk through nature, and you will see His love surrounding you. Is there anything we have that didn't come from God? He knows what we need before we ask.

> *"Every good gift and every perfect gift is from above, and comes down from the Father of lights, with whom there is no variation or shadow of turning" (James 1:17).*

Love Through Service

Service is the hardest way for me to receive love. I don't want others to do for me. I want to do it all myself. I want to be in control. But at the end of my rope when I can't do it anymore, He picks me up and does it for me. He meets my every need.

When I published my book on prayer, *Pearls: 5 Essentials for a Richer Prayer Life*, I told God I would be blessed and encouraged if it helped just one person. Somewhere in the publishing and promotion, I began to look for the praise of others and more book sales. One time when I was discouraged, a lady I didn't know well shared with me that my book had totally revolutionized her prayer life. God reminded me in that moment what it was all about. That was all I needed. The pouring of words onto the page is all about glorifying God and hoping those words help others grow closer to Him.

God may send others to serve us or in our place when we come up short. We need to open our eyes to service around us. Ask Him to show you.

Love through Touch

He has touched my life in so many moments. In Scripture we see those He touched physically as well as the lives touched emotionally and spiritually. In my lowest moments of disappointment and regret, I have felt His presence as if He wrapped His arms around me. He put the pieces of my shattered heart back together and built a wall of protection around it through His love manifested in His Word.

Love One Another

No matter how you best communicate or receive love, there are still specific commandments God gives concerning how to show our love to Him and to others. Our method to love is like spiritual gifts. When I take a spiritual gift test, mercy is always low on mine; however, God's Word tells me I am called to be merciful. While it may not come naturally, it's something I must do. In seeking the ability to be merciful, I grow closer to God, because I can't do it alone. It's the same with showing love. While we may inherently operate under one or two styles of communicating love, the Holy Spirit makes it possible to show love to others in ways that may not come naturally.

We are also commanded to love one another. But we aren't left high and dry not knowing how. Scripture either tells us how or shows us how by example.

> *"A new commandment I give to you,*
> *that you love one another; as I have loved you,*
> *that you also love one another" (John 13:34).*

The command is to love one another. The how is as Christ loved us.

> *"Let no corrupt word proceed out of your mouth,*
> *but what is good for necessary edification,*
> *that it may impart grace to the hearers" (Ephesians 4:29).*

The command is to love one another. The how is through edification and words of grace.

In Mark 6:31-34 Jesus and the disciples are tired and need rest; but out of compassion, He continues to teach and minister.

The command is to love one another. The how is through time, even when you don't feel like it.

"Be kindly affectionate to one another with brotherly love, in honor giving preference to one another" (Romans 12:10).

The command is to love one another. The how is by giving preference to one another.

"Then Peter said, 'Silver and gold I do not have, but what I do have I give you: In the name of Jesus Christ of Nazareth, rise up and walk'" (Acts 3:6).

The command is to love one another. The how is by giving what we have either through our spiritual gifts or out of the abundance of how He has blessed us.

"For you, brethren, have been called to liberty; only do not use liberty as an opportunity for the flesh, but through love serve one another" (Galatians 5:13).

The command is to love one another. The how is by serving one another.

"Then Jesus, moved with compassion, stretched out His hand and touched him, and said to him, 'I am willing; be cleansed'" (Mark 1:41).

The command is to love one another. The how is through a compassionate touch. Jesus didn't have to touch the man to heal him, but He knew what the man needed.

We may have to ask God how we can show His love to others. It could be a kind word, time to listen, a gift, doing repairs or making meals, or maybe a hug.

There is a lady in my office who I believe has a dual love language of words of affirmation and gifts. She does a good job, and I do my best to spend some time with her each day, though not much is required. What she does respond to is others telling her she does a good job or a gift of appreciation. For this lady, I could offer to help her with her work or spend more time with her every day, but those don't mean as much as the recognition and token gifts of appreciation. There are times that one expression of love may be needed more than others. I wouldn't hug this lady every day, but when her mom was sick, she needed a compassionate touch.

Giving and Receiving Love

The book of Ruth tells us about the need for love by both a woman named Naomi and her daughter-in-law, Ruth. Naomi and her sons went with her husband as they left home for another country. In the years she was there, her husband died. Her sons grew up and married women from this foreign country. Then tragedy struck and both of her sons died. Naomi was left alone and decided to return home. One of her daughters-in-law, Ruth, insisted on going with her. Ruth had lost her husband, but she made the decision to leave her country and follow Naomi. She chose to love Naomi and follow Naomi's God. She gave love to Naomi out of what surely had to be her own need for love.

Upon returning to Naomi's homeland, Ruth worked to feed them both by gleaning in the barley fields. There she found the favor of a man named Boaz. They ended up getting married. Her own need for love was met out of her choice to love another. The greatest legacy from this story is that Ruth also carries the lineage to the Messiah through Boaz. What greater long-term future reward could there be?

Love is like a circle represented by a ring with no beginning and no end. This is perfect love. And the only perfect love is in Christ. God shows His love to us however we need it, so what is God's love language? How do we love Him well? According to Scripture it is our obedience.

"If you love Me, keep My commandments" (John 14:15).

In the next chapter, we will look at this circle of love and how we show our love for Him through obedience.

Treasure Hunt

Read 1 Corinthians 13. What treasure do you find here? Remember that these are traits of God's love that we cannot manufacture or produce on our own. They are the fruit of our relationship with Christ and nourishment from God's Word.

11

Circle of Love

"We love, because He first loved us" (1 John 4:19 NASB).

A few years ago, I completed a discipleship course at church. One of the assignments was to tell God we loved Him three times every hour, every day. It surprised me when I realized I didn't normally tell God that I loved Him. I thanked Him regularly but saying "I love You" to God seemed strange, and I wondered why. Of course I love God, so why wasn't this a normal practice? What does it mean to love God?

I remembered the discussions about love that Mr. Wonderful and I had before getting married. We talked about how the infatuation of new love would wear off. We discussed that loving someone is a choice, a decision. I choose to love Mr. Wonderful. On days when things don't go right and he does something that irritates me (although this never happens), I still love him. If Mr. Wonderful stopped loving me or no longer showed his love for me, I would have a choice to make. Do I love him because of what he does for me and how he treats me? Or do I love him because I have made a choice and a commitment to love him?

Scripture says, "We love Him because He first loved us" (NKJV). This doesn't mean we love God because He is good or shows us love, but it means that God has made it possible for us to love at all.

Consider how we act when we love someone. When we fall in love, all we think about is the one we are in love with. When Mr. Wonderful and I were dating, we stayed up late at night talking on the phone. Many nights we sacrificed our sleep just to hear each other's voice. When we were first married, we did everything together: errands like the dry cleaners, the drug store, grocery store, hardware store, the mall, hobbies we had individually enjoyed before, even yard work. We wanted to be together and put the other one's wishes above our own. We desired each other's presence and wanted to hear their voice. Considering this kind of love toward God, we can ask several questions.

- When was the last time I missed sleep so I could stay up and spend time with God? While I've done this on occasion, it's usually during a time of crisis.

- Do I think about God incessantly? Yes and no. My goal is a 24/7 relationship. Yes, God is with me every day, hour, minute, and second, but I want to constantly be in His presence as a state of my mind. The more time I spend with Him, the more I think about Him during the day. I find myself thanking God throughout the day for things like a good parking spot, an easy merge in traffic, and a problem solved at work. There was a time I would remember these little things after the fact or not at all. I want to be aware in the moment how God blesses me each day.

- Do I desire His presence everywhere I go and long to hear His voice? Easy answer is yes, but this requires thought as to where I go and the willingness to listen for His voice in those circumstances.

- What sacrifices am I willing to make for God in comparison to the sacrifices I make for my family because I love them? I'll gladly miss a TV show or put down a book I'm reading to see my grandkids' school or sporting events. Will I do the same to spend time with God?

- What is the first thing I think about in the morning? Usually the sound of the alarm and whether or not to hit snooze is my first thought. A few minutes later a Christian radio station begins to play. This places a song of praise in my mind as I begin my morning routine.

- Do my thoughts naturally go to God with a desire to talk to Him (otherwise known as prayer) and read His words? Again, the more time I spend with Him, the more this happens. It's that second nature principle from Chapter 4.

- Where is my comfort? Is it in God alone or in flowers, chocolate, jewelry, shoes, or my favorite restaurant?

Do I really love God? Do you? How do we develop this love?

First, it's a command. Jesus said this was the greatest commandment, to love the Lord your God with all your heart, soul, mind, and strength (Mark 12:30). Our heart is our center, our thoughts, our feelings. Our soul is our very breath and who we are. Our mind refers to our understanding and intellect; thus, not a blind faith, but a decision to love. Our strength is our ability and might. It's an intense love. Loving God with all our heart, soul, mind, and strength combines the innermost part of who we are, our decisions, and the strength to act.

Second, Jesus said to keep His commandments. "If you love me, keep my commandments" (John 14:15). It's like a circle. We are commanded to love Him. And if we love Him, we keep His commandments—one of which is loving Him. Obedience is part of love.

You've probably heard the question, which came first – the chicken or the egg? I pose the question, which came first - love or obedience? In the beginning God created, so I would say the chicken came before the egg. In the beginning God loved us first, so I would say love came before obedience. But either one works. Whether we start by choosing to love out of obedience or start by obeying out of love, we will find ourselves in the circle with no beginning or end. It doesn't matter where we jump on. It only matters that we do. Love. Obedience. Love. The circle of love. We show our love for God through His love language, which is our obedience.

All My Heart

We are commanded to love God, and Scripture tells us how. We love God with all our heart. My favorite chapter in the Bible is Psalm 119. Six times the Psalmist says he loves God with his whole heart.

The word *whole* means something has been made complete or perfect. The whole as all, any, or every—the whole thing. The word heart refers to our heart as the most interior organ and is used widely for our feelings. It's also used to indicate the center of something. The complete center of our being. According to *Vine's Concise Dictionary of Bible Words,* "The word used for heart in the Old Testament often means the inner person, with a focus on the psychological aspects of the mind and heart, which also includes decision making ability."[1] This brings us back to our love being a decision that results in our obedience.

We are to love God with our whole heart or with the complete center of our being. From the inside out. If you have ever had a hot flash (showing my age now), you have a greater understanding of this. A hot flash isn't the same as getting hot from being outside in the sun or in a hot room. A hot flash comes from the inside. It starts from the center of your being and radiates outward. It's from the inside out.

A hot flash is an internal, hormonally triggered sensation. It's an inside job. The exact cause of hot flashes isn't known, but the signs and symptoms point to factors affecting the function of your body's thermostat — the hypothalamus. This area at the base of your brain regulates body temperature and other basic processes. The estrogen reduction you experience during menopause may disrupt hypothalamic function, leading to hot flashes.[2]

Thank you, God, for letting me experience hot flashes, so I can have a better understanding of what it means to love you from the complete center of my being, inside out.

Deuteronomy 10:12-13 "And now, Israel, what does the Lord your God require of you, but to fear the Lord your God, to walk in all His ways and to love Him, to serve the Lord your God with all your heart and with all your soul, and to keep the commandments of the Lord and His statutes."

Unmasked

During the health pandemic of 2020, the CDC recommended we all wear masks to protect ourselves and others. Masks soon became a new fashion accessory. People would wear masks that looked funny, supported a political opinion, claimed their faith, or noted their opposition of being told what to do. This reminded me of the masks we already wear every day. Many Christians wear a mask that looks like love on the outside. We play a part to convince others of something insincere. God knows what is behind our mask, but do we realize we are wearing one? Ask these questions.

- What percent of my money do I spend where? Pull up your online bank statement and sort it by item. Look at where your money goes. How much is necessity versus luxury versus God's leading? It's all His, so how are we stewarding His money? I'm not condemning luxury, only suggesting we give our desire for it our attention.

- What percent of my time do I spend where? I've read many books on becoming more organized or planning your time well. They all suggest a time log. Keep a log this week or take time now to review this past week. Diagram your time. How much is business, how much is personal, how much involves your family, and how much is really devoted to God?

- If what I do is an overflow of what is in my heart, what do my actions say about my heart?

Each question is a cause for reflection on who we really are. In my self-examination, I cried out to God about the selfishness I found in my own heart and asked him to replace it with His love for others. The next morning, He showed me this verse that I am clinging to as I look to Him. "God gave him another heart" (1 Samuel 10:9). I am trusting God for His heart as I walk with Him. I am learning to love Him more every day and allow His love to reflect from my heart unmasked.

Are you wearing a mask? The mask I'm referring to doesn't hide our face, but our heart. Take off the mask and ask God to give you another heart.

Walk in the Comfort of Ruby Slippers

You never know for sure what your feet are really getting into when you buy a new pair of shoes. They can feel comfortable walking around the store, but the real test for me is whether or not I can wear them to the grocery store after a full day at work. I'm known to run around my office barefoot after 5:00, but the errands when I leave still require shoes. They need to take me to work, help me run errands, and then get me home.

We all remember Dorothy in *The Wizard of Oz*. She walked down the yellow brick road because she was looking for a way home. What she didn't realize was that she had the ability to go home at any time. She just didn't know it. She was walking in the ruby slippers that gave her a way home.

According to Ephesians 2:10, "We are His workmanship, created in Christ Jesus for good works, which God prepared beforehand, that we should walk in them." God wants us to walk in the good works He has prepared for each of us individually. To walk this path, He provides ruby slippers designed just for you. Whether yours are pumps or flips flops, they are covered in rubies of His love. They fit perfectly and give a cushion to your step. They don't pinch, rub, or slip. They are designed for you to walk in His love comfortably. God's ruby slippers also show us the way home by loving God through obedience.

Last year my feet began having problems. My heels hurt, my feet turned red and swelled, and it hurt to walk. I made an appointment with a foot and ankle specialist at the orthopedist. The first thing he did was x-ray my feet. He said I had high arches, diagnosed plantar fasciitis, and noted extreme inflammation throughout both feet. He also said the bones on the side of my right foot were close to having a stress fracture. His recommendation was to wear tennis shoes with support until I got better. Stop wearing shoes without support, and pretty much nix the high heels or a stress fracture would put me in a boot.

Anyone who knows me well knows I don't wear tennis shoes unless walking for exercise. My feet like to breathe. I have a love-hate relationship with shoes of any type. I love cute shoes, but I prefer to go barefoot. I also love a good bargain, so spending money on more expensive shoes with the required support and looking like an old lady was contrary to my nature. Fortunately, not all shoes with support are made for old women, which I refuse to admit becoming. I found cute shoes supporting high arches and can still work in my previous cute shoes from time to time. But the three-inch-plus heels have gone by the wayside, most days.

What makes a shoe the right fit? They don't pinch your toes, don't rub blisters on your heel, don't slip off, and are comfortable. Oh, and in my case, they provide support to high arches. In the same way, God has a purpose for our walk with Him that is perfectly designed for our feet. He has placed abilities in us that we may not see. To walk in our designated path, we need our ruby slippers to be exactly the right fit. And they are when we are wearing the rubies God has planned for us.

Everything you need to walk in the good works planned for you, God will provide. Just click your heels three times. Pray, pray, pray. Ask Him for what you need, listen to what He says, and act on what He tells you. Remember, there's no place like home. If you have wandered off the path God has for you, pull those ruby slippers out of your spiritual jewelry box, come back home, and rest in the arms of God. He is the God of all comfort. Walk in the good works He has prepared for you.

Walk in Love

"And we know that for those who love God all things work together for good, for those who are called according to his purpose" (Romans 8:28 ESV).

All things work together for good. It doesn't say all things ARE good. All things work TOGETHER for good with two assumptions.

1. For those who love God.

2. For those called according to His purpose.

All things working together for our good is predicated on the fact that we love God and as Christians are called according to God's purpose. As we looked at earlier, our love for God is shown by our obedience to God according to His commandments.

"This is love, that we walk according to His commandments.

This is the commandment, that as you have heard from the
beginning, you should walk in it" (2 John 1:6).

Love is a desire to be first in someone's life. Other than usurping the place of God, don't we all want to be first place in someone's life? As a wife, I want to be first in my husband's life. As a mom with young children, I wanted to have first place in my children's lives. This changed when they got married and is why, as a mom, it is sometimes so hard to let go. We must accept the fact that we are no longer first in their lives. Loving others is putting them above ourselves.

"Let nothing be done through selfish ambition or conceit, but
in lowliness of mind let each esteem others better than himself.
Let each of you look out not only for his own interests, but also
for the interests of others" (Philippians 2:3-4).

"A new commandment I give to you, that you love one another.
Just as I have loved you, you also are to love one another. By
this all people will know that you are my disciples, if you have
love for one another" (John 13:34-35).

In other words (my take on this): Love one another!

When we love God, He gives us the ability to love others. Loving God unlocks the door of our heart to allow His love to enter. When we love God, we want to do what He wants. We abide in Him, then we grow in Him, and then we produce fruit. Ever want more peace, love, and joy? Ever want more patience, kindness, and gentleness? Ever want more goodness, faithfulness, and self-control? These are the fruit of the Spirit produced in our lives when we walk with Him.

When I first began telling God I loved Him by saying the words, it was stilted. The more I told Him how much I loved Him from deep in my heart, the easier it came from my mouth. At some point it became a natural expression from my heart. I resolve to love God. It is my resolution from this point forward. It is my choice. It is my decision. What about you?

Treasure Hunt

Read 1 John and mark every reference to God's love and loving Him. Which ones speak to you the loudest?

Amethysts of Peace

Introduction

In the middle of a divorce. That word carries such emotions. While some may throw it around without a thought like just another way to change your circumstances, to me it meant failure. It meant I couldn't fix it. It meant the end of a dream I believed was from God.

Lost in my work. He knew where I worked, but he also knew better than to show up at my office. At work I could forget my problems. Except for the phone calls. They wouldn't stop. They were disrupting my concentration on my tasks, and they were disrupting others at my workplace. Finally, our receptionist saved the day. She knew his voice. So when he called, she said I wasn't available. Bless her.

Sleep. Blissful sleep and rest. As I drifted into the rest that only seemed to come when I was asleep, the shrill ringing invaded my slumber. He wouldn't stop calling. This was before cell phones and cordless phones. It was before call block. It must have been before private numbers, or I somehow missed that option. My phone also didn't have a switch to turn off the ringer. The only solution was to unplug the cord from the wall. This sounds like an easy option, but I also worried about him finding out where I lived and my need to call for help. My phone was a lifeline to help, and he was controlling that too.

Even after it was all over and he married someone else, the calls kept coming. Peace. I needed peace, and God gave me peace beyond my understanding. I could rest in Him alone.

I had to unplug from uncertain and unreliable rest. I had to let God restore my soul and give me His fiery peace.

12

He Restores My Soul

"The Lord is my shepherd . . . He restores my soul"
(Psalm 23:1, 3).

Mr. Wonderful and I love antiquing. It's not only antique fur-
niture we look for, but items that bring back memories, like
my grandmother's dishes. I especially love some of the old
wooden boxes we have found that I use for everything from
shelving towels to potting plants. Mr. Wonderful collects old
clocks, radios, and fans.

Our favorite store is owned by a couple from Maine. A few
times each year they travel to Maine and bring back a truckload
from old barns. They don't repair their finds, and that's where
our fun begins. We restore and repurpose. Mr. Wonderful has
developed a talent for bringing these items back to life. One
of my favorites is the two triple sewing drawers from an old
sewing machine. He connected them and made a top from

reclaimed chestnut that he found in North Carolina. The restored sewing drawers now sit on a table in my sewing/craft room and hold thread and sewing items. Another is a square four-drawer library card file that sits next to our coffee maker organizing coffee pods, creamers, and sugars. Great find.

Restoration is returning something to a former owner, place, or condition. When something is restored, it is turned back. We pick up antiques and repurpose them, but God wants to restore us and return us to our original purpose. Adam and Eve walked in perfect fellowship with God. When sin entered the world, that perfect fellowship was lost. Jesus came to make restoration possible. He didn't come to repurpose us, but to restore original fellowship.

Lost

Like the old hymn says, I once was lost but now am found.

Luke 15 begins with a crowd drawing near to hear Jesus speak. He tells three parables of the lost sheep, lost coin, and lost son. The parable of the lost sheep explains the heart of a shepherd for one lost sheep in his flock and the rejoicing experienced once found. The parable of the lost coin shows a diligent search by a woman like what a woman now might experience if she lost the diamond from her wedding ring. In both parables Jesus compares them to joy in heaven over one sinner who repents.

The parable of the lost son reminds me that I am already a child of God, yet I sin. When I return and ask God's forgiveness, He forgives. He doesn't punish. He has compassion covering me with grace and mercy. He sees me, and He restores me. Like the older brother in this parable, sometimes as

Christians we judge others when God blesses them. But verse 31 reminds us that all God has belongs to us as we walk with Him.

In each parable something is lost and then found. In verses 24 and 32, the father says of his son that he was dead and is alive again. To be made alive again is to be restored to a correct life.

The definition of the Greek word used for lost in these parables means to destroy, render useless, or to lose. John 10:10 uses the same word, but it is translated as destroy when it says, "The thief comes only to steal, kill, and destroy" (ESV). When I walk away from God's path, I get lost, and I am rendered useless. I am allowing Satan to destroy me.

The second half of John 10:10 is a contrast to the first. Jesus says, "I came that they may have life and have it abundantly." This is more than basic life. He gives life more abundant – exceeding measure, more than necessary (not just the basics), surpassing, superabundant. Absolute fullness of life is the opposite of loss and destruction.

Another contrast is in Luke 9:56 where Jesus says, "The Son of Man did not come to destroy men's lives, but to save them." The word save means to rescue from danger or destruction.

Psalm 23:3 says, "He restores my soul." When God restores my soul, He turns it back to Him. I am restored to Him and made righteous through Him. The death, burial, and resurrection of Christ restores us to our original design. He gives us a new purpose for life. When we find ourselves scuffed and broken and we no longer feel useful, He restores us. He gives us new life and purpose through restoration to our original design. When I am off course, He brings me back.

We were made for a relationship with God. Sin separated us. The cross restored that relationship. What was once an old dirty box is now home to a beautiful plant in my kitchen window. What was once a broken crate sitting flat on the bottom now reveals lustrous wood and stands vertically holding washcloths in my bathroom. What was once a broken young woman who had lost her original purpose now radiates God's beauty from her spiritual jewelry box.

Peace in Rest

During disappointing seasons of life, some days I want to sleep and block out the emotional hurts. I'm searching for peace. There is no pain in sleep. It brings peace. When I wake up after a good night's sleep, things always seem easier to deal with. God created us to need sleep. During sleep our bodies restore and repair our cells.

Studies show different stages of sleep. Philip Gehrman, Ph.D., assistant professor of psychiatry at the University of Pennsylvania, dubs stage two sleep "average sleep"—it's not too deep, not too light, and it's where you spend about half the night.[1] This reminds me of Goldilocks. Not too hot and not too cold. Just right.

As you move into stage two sleep, you lose a sense of your surroundings and your body temp drops. Gehrman says of stage three, "This is our deepest sleep." During this restorative stage of sleep, blood pressure drops, breathing slows down, blood flow moves to the muscles, and tissue is repaired according to the National Sleep Foundation. "Since this is the deepest sleep (and the one that makes you feel well-rested and energetic the next day), it's also the hardest stage to be woken from," Gehrman says.[2]

There is nothing better than a restful night's sleep. One night I woke up to a loud noise. I shook and pushed Mr. Wonderful until he woke up. The security alarm in the house was sounding. He jumped out of bed and told me to stay put. Then he took off around the house half-dressed, checking all the doors and asking me which station was blinking on the alarm pad. At the same time, the security company called to see if everything was all right or if they should dispatch help. Looking back, it was quite comical. As he yelled to ask which station, the security company was telling me which station. I could see on the panel it was station five, but still groggy from sleep I couldn't recall what that meant.

Turns out it was the fire alarm. Mr. Wonderful checked the house and went up in the attic. No fire. No visual smoke. Not even the smell of smoke. He checked the batteries in our smoke detectors, I reset the alarm panel, and we went back to bed. After three more times being violently aroused to the same alarm, a dispatch supervisor called and explained that this had nothing to do with our individual smoke detectors. The security panel was triggered by the main fire alarm tied into the system. She couldn't tell me where the main detector was located, only that it would look different from the others. I remembered (now that I was sufficiently awake) a contraption on the ceiling at the top of the stairs. Mr. Wonderful climbed a ladder to check the strange looking contraption and change the battery, but there was no battery. Thankfully, he is handy at home things and knew how to disconnect the wires. No more alarms that night. It wasn't until later I realized we hadn't set our alarm that night, so an intruder couldn't have set it off.

When the unexpected comes, it interrupts our second nature expectations and can bring confusion. In the same way our sleep was interrupted, disappointments bring unrest and confusion. In our case above, sleep was lost but restored the next night. In life's disappointments, much more is lost. The only way to combat this is through God's restoration of what was lost. In Joel 2, God promised His people that He would restore to them what they had lost. He said they would know that He was in their midst, that He is the Lord God and there is no other. When we seek and trust God for our restoration, He restores our loss and shows up in the middle of the chaos. God gets the glory for restoration.

Other People's Sins

Disappointments in life can be caused by our own mistakes or from circumstances of life beyond our control like the destruction of a tornado. They also come about when our dreams are shattered because of someone else's sins. What happens when our world is turned upside down because of someone else? The story of Bathsheba is a good example.[3]

We usually view this story from David's point of view, which follows Scripture. But stop and think about her side. How did she feel? For some reason I always view the story of David and Bathsheba after the great sin and the consequences that followed. I have always imagined they went on to be the perfect married couple with her giving birth to Solomon who would be the next king, build the temple, and be the lineage of Jesus.

It might have felt flattering to be desired by the king, but it cost her sorrow. She lost her husband. Then she lost her child. Whether expressed or not, she surely blamed David for her loss. It would be hard to forgive. The grave disappointment would certainly cause turmoil. She lost her husband and her baby because of David's sin. Her life was affected by his adultery, murder, and the loss of their child. But peace came through restoration and the promises of God.

God promised that her next child would be the lineage to the Messiah. That's a more desirable honor, looking forward to her son as a king versus her husband as king. While David was a man after God's own heart, I often wonder if Bathsheba wasn't in the same court. Could she have been a woman after God's heart? Scripture doesn't say, but we can glean that it is possible to experience peace again through the forgiveness she must have given to David.

Sometimes our lives are affected by someone else's sin. In my first marriage, my dreams were shattered by the effects of alcohol, abuse, and adultery. My expectations were not met, and the rug was pulled out from under me. My dreams fell flat. It seemed everything was lost.

A friend recently asked if I had forgiven my first husband. Sometimes that's a hard question to answer. My quick answer has always been yes, but I came to realize the cliché "out of sight, out of mind" contributed to my answer. After not seeing him for years, I didn't give him a thought. Since I didn't feel bitter and felt almost nothing toward him, I considered that forgiveness; but I wasn't sure how to know. How would I react if I ran into him somewhere unexpectedly?

A couple of scenarios came to mind. The first was making sure he didn't notice me or hoping he wouldn't recognize me. I could pretend to be someone else. I didn't want to see him or confront the past. The second scenario was slapping the living daylights out of him for all he did to me. Neither scenario seemed to reflect forgiveness. It wasn't until I could picture coming face to face with him and either shaking his hand or giving him a small hug and asking how he was doing these days that I realized forgiveness.

Sometimes forgiveness is an ongoing process that must happen over and over. If someone you need to forgive is active in your life, can you pray blessings for them? Can you have compassion and extend mercy? These are different ways to help know if you have forgiven. Ask God to give you an example of how you can know for sure.

Consider Joseph. We often focus on how he endured circumstances beyond his control. Many of these circumstances were caused by other people's sins. His brothers sold him into slavery. Potiphar's wife tried to seduce him and lied about his character, and the baker was so caught up in his own restoration that he forgot about Joseph for two years. There is no record of Joseph feeling animosity against any of these people. We never see him discouraged. He moves forward doing his best, no matter the situation. He just seems perfect, and he even forgives his own brothers. Odds are good that he struggled with the question of why. But Scripture records a life of peace in adversity. His peace was possible because of his faith in God and his ability to forgive because of that faith.

If our disappointments come from our own sins, we need to be able to forgive ourselves first. But when our disappointments come from someone else's sin, the next step is forgiving them. Only in learning to forgive can we experience peace.

Peace in Forgiveness

Ephesians 4:32 says we are to forgive others as God in Christ forgave us. Whatever sins we have committed have been forgiven. We many times forget this scripture applies to others. Any sin someone has committed against us, they have also committed against God. Yet He offers forgiveness. He loves us, and He loves them the same. Christ died for us, and He died for them the same. He offered Himself for our forgiveness, and He offered Himself for their forgiveness. Because of this, we can forgive others, but we can't do it on our own. We do it through understanding God's forgiveness, allowing Him to soften our hearts, and allowing His forgiveness through us.

The parable in Matthew 18:23-24 tells the story of a man owing an enormous debt to the king. He pleaded for patience and mercy, and the king forgave the full debt to everyone's astonishment. But then this man who was forgiven so much went to a fellow servant who owed him little in comparison and demanded payment, even going so far as to have the man thrown into prison. Everyone was once again astonished, and some told the king what happened. The king was furious and took what the first man had and threw him in prison. We feel justified at the first man's sentence. After all, he was shown compassion yet exhibited none himself. We react the same way to this parable, yet aren't we sometimes just as guilty? Jesus paid for our debt, yet we hold others accountable to pay their sin debts to us.

Rachael Denhollander, the former gymnast who became the first woman to publicly accuse Larry Nassar of sexual abuse, spoke directly to Larry Nassar during the sentencing phase of his trial for criminal sexual conduct. Part of her statement reads, *"I pray you experience the soul crushing weight of guilt so you may someday experience true repentance and true forgiveness from God, which you need far more than forgiveness from me -- though I extend that to you as well."*[4]

How can such forgiveness be extended except through the forgiveness in Christ? Sin angers me. My own sin and that of others. Unforgiveness brings additional sin to my life. It destroys my peace. I must take this to God so that He can restore my peace through His forgiveness.

Times of Refreshing

I love the peace of a gentle, steady rain. I feel a time of refreshing, a time of nourishing, and a time of meeting needs (one of which is a lower water bill when we get summer rains).

But just like when the rains turn into floods and overtake the floodgates and dams created to hold them back, when God fills us, we need to release the floodgates and let His peace overflow to the situations and people around us.

"You visit the earth and water it, You greatly enrich it ...
You make it soft with showers, You bless its growth"
(Psalm 65:9-10).

His Word enriches us, softens are heart, and blesses our growth.

Psalm 23, a Psalm of David

"The Lord is my shepherd; I shall not want.
He makes me to lie down in green pastures; He leads me beside the still waters.
He restores my soul; He leads me in the paths of righteousness for His name's sake.

Yea, though I walk through the valley of the shadow of
death, I will fear no evil;
For You are with me; Your rod and Your staff, they comfort
me.

You prepare a table before me in the presence of my
enemies;
You anoint my head with oil; My cup runs over.
Surely goodness and mercy shall follow me all the days of
my life;
And I will dwell in the house of the Lord forever."

In verse 1, David says, "The Lord is my shepherd." He didn't
say the Lord is my tentmaker or the Lord is my builder. He
had firsthand experience in being a shepherd. He knew what
a shepherd did and how a shepherd cared for his sheep. God
was David's shepherd because David understood shepherds.

Most of us have been taught about a shepherd and his
sheep to help us understand the continual references throughout scripture. But what if David wasn't a shepherd? What other analogy might he have used? If David had been a farmer
instead of a shepherd, do you think Psalm 23 would read
differently?

I know what my role is at work and where my strengths are
in everyday life. The Lord is not only my shepherd (because
I have learned what that means); He is also my manager, my
planner, my organizer, my project manager, and my life con-
troller. These are areas that I know firsthand. What is God to
you? I challenge you to write this for yourself. Is God your
financial planner, protector, home manager, teacher, helper,
dispatcher, or guide? Sometimes the hardest area to surrender

to God is the area we know best, but God speaks to us individually where we are and understands what we need.

Here is one way this speaks to me:

The Lord controls my life, I shall not worry. He makes me sleep peacefully at night.
He leads me beside fulfillment. He restores my soul.
He leads me down paths He has prepared because He knows best.
Even though I walk through the valley of the unknown,
I will not fear, for You are with me.
Your omniscient GPS and Your compass comfort me.
You prepare a plan before me in the presence of the chaos around me.
You anoint me with love, and my heart overflows.
Surely goodness and mercy shall follow me all the days of my life,
And I shall dwell in the house of the Lord forever.

What is your career, or what are your strengths? Let God be those things to you, just as God was a shepherd to David. Let go of where you think you can do it on your own. Surrender that area to God. In surrender, you will find His peace, and He will restore your soul.

Treasure Hunt

Read Psalm 23 in three different versions. Rewrite it where it speaks to you best.

13

Fiery Peace

"You will keep him in perfect peace, Whose mind is stayed on you, because he trusts You" (Isaiah 26:3).

The tornado sirens blared, and I began pulling things out of the closet under the stairs. The experts always say an interior room on the first floor with no windows is the safest place to be. Our closet in the middle of the house would be the safest place if the tornado came our way. At 3:00 in the afternoon, it was dark as night, but we could hear the winds. When the lightning flashed, we could see the trees bending sideways. Into the closet we went. After several minutes huddled under the stairs, the sirens stopped and the howling winds passed. Peace.

Living in Texas, this wasn't the first time I sat in a closet waiting for a storm to pass. But this day brought me back to a passage I had read that morning in Jeremiah. While the storm raged outside, I sought peace in the closet. Once the storm passed, I was free to return to life as normal.

In Jeremiah 27-29, Israel was under Babylonian rule by King Nebuchadnezzar. False prophets had been telling the people not to submit to the king of Babylon. Then the prophet Jeremiah sent a letter to those carried away captive giving them truth from God.

God told them to build houses, to dwell in them, to plant gardens, and to raise their families. He told them to seek the peace of the city where they were held captive, for in that city's peace they would have peace. He promised them they would return home, but not until after seventy years.

It was in our closet under the stairs that God spoke to me about seeking peace wherever I find myself until God says move. Sometimes I pray for God to remove a circumstance in my life, but His plan might be for me to find peace within that circumstance for a time. I should pray for peace in the circumstance, not always for removal from that circumstance.

God had a timetable for Israel. It was seventy years. He had a plan. Verse 12 says, "Then you will call upon Me and go and pray to Me, and I will listen to you. And you will seek Me and find Me, when you search for Me with all your heart. I will be found by you, says the Lord, and I will bring you back from your captivity." But not a moment too soon.

I have learned in my captive circumstances to focus on God and His words. I pray for peace, and in God's timing He brings me home. But not a moment too soon. I continue to seek Him and search for Him with all my heart, and I have found that He can still give peace during the tough times. Circumstances don't have to disappear to have His peace.

In Jeremiah they were to live in their circumstance and seek peace there. They were also to pray, seek God, and search for Him with all their heart.

Amethysts

The purple Amethyst has been highly esteemed throughout the ages for its stunning beauty and legendary powers to stimulate and soothe the mind and emotions. It is a semi-precious stone in today's classifications, but to the ancients it was a "Gem of Fire," a precious stone worth as much as a diamond at certain times.[1]

As a gem of fire, it can also represent peace.

Fiery Peace

There are many references to fire in the Bible. Sometimes fire is the result of chaos such as in Sodom and Gomorrah and results in destruction. The fire of hell is the worst. Other times it ushers in peace either immediately or right after the fire and brings healing.

- 1 Corinthians says our works will be tested by fire for their purity.
- 1 Peter 1:7 references being tried by fire.
- God spoke to Moses from fire in the burning bush.
- The Israelites were led in the desert by a pillar of fire by night.
- Elijah challenged the prophets of Baal, and fire fell from heaven consuming the sacrifice.

- Later Elijah stood on a mountain and waited for God's revelation. There was a strong wind, then an earthquake, and then a fire. But God spoke to him in a still small voice.

- Pentecost was signified by the appearance of tongues of fire on the apostles as they waited for the Holy Spirit.

A great example of peace in the middle of fire is Shadrach, Meshach, and Abednego.[2] These three men were faithful to God and refused to worship the image of gold set up by the king at that time. The edict was that anyone who didn't bow before the image would be cast into a burning fiery furnace. When the king found out these three men didn't bow and worship the gold image, he was furious, but he gave them one more chance. He asked them who would save them from his hands. Their answer was, "Our God whom we serve is able to deliver us." Then the king ordered they be thrown in the furnace.

I can't imagine that these three men had total peace at that time. They knew God was able to save them, but they stated that even if He didn't, they still would not worship another god. They stood firm in worship of the one true God, but they were probably battling fear within. Everything changed when they were thrown in the fire. The king immediately noticed they were walking around unharmed. And then he saw a fourth figure. They walked in the fire with Jesus, and I can only imagine the sweet peace in that moment.

Have you ever had a sunburn? The sun is millions of miles away from earth and can do painful damage to our skin. Imagine the pain of being burned by direct contact with fire. Scripture tells us that the fire had no power over these three men. Their hair was not singed, and the fire did not leave a smell on them. The result of this was glory to God, not these men. The king declared, "There is no other God who can deliver like this."

In Philippians we are told not to be anxious (live within our circumstance and seek peace there) and to pray. Philippians 4:7 says, "The peace of God which surpasses all understanding, will guard your hearts and minds through Christ Jesus." The Blue Letter Bible describes this peace as an exemption from the rage and havoc of war.[3] Walking in the fire yet exempt from the damage it can do. This peace rises above any circumstance we can walk through and guards our hearts and minds because Jesus Christ walks with us.

Short of Peace

Short. That's me. I am short of stature, barely over five feet tall. I've climbed shelves at the grocery store to reach items on the top shelf more than once. People look at me like I'm crazy, so sometimes I ask for their help. I've yet to be told no. I take twice as many steps as Mr. Wonderful when we go for a walk, and I pull my seat up all the way in the car when I drive. Yes, I'm short.

Luke 19 records the story of a man named Zacchaeus who was also short of stature. He was trying to see Jesus in the crowd, but he was too short, so he climbed a tree for a better view. Kind of like climbing those shelves at the grocery store, but the tree was probably more stable.

Scripture says he sought to see Jesus. He wasn't willing to just let Him pass by. He was determined to see Him and get a glimpse of who He was. Jesus saw Zacchaeus in the tree, but I believe Jesus would have seen him in the crowd. He told Zacchaeus to come down. He met him where he was, short of stature.

You may not be short of stature physically, but we all go through times when we are short of peace. When we seek Him through prayer, He will meet us where we are, despite our shortcomings.

The question isn't whether I'm willing to climb the shelves or ask for help. It's not what I can do to reach up and be closer to heaven. None of us can reach up high enough to heaven. That's why Jesus reaches down to us. The better question is, *Am I seeking Him?*

He sees us where we are. He lifts us up when we are stuck in our sins or stuck in confusion or stuck in disappointment. He sees us when we are paralyzed in fear and when we feel alone. We climb the trees (or shelves in my case) to get a better view. We climb the church ladder and the good works ladder, but Jesus says come down.

Zacchaeus sought Him the only way he knew. Are we seeking Him? The physical climbs are not what He wants. The spiritual seeking of our heart is what He wants. It's there He meets us, extends His hand, and gathers us to His side. It is there we find peace.

> *"For You do not desire sacrifice, or else I would give it; You do not delight in burnt offering. The sacrifices of God are a broken spirit, a broken and contrite heart – These, O God, You will not despise" (Psalm 51:16-17).*

Telescopic Focus

As we seek peace, we need a focus on God. Not just a general focus but a telescopic focus.

A telescope is an optical instrument used to magnify and enhance the view of faraway objects, be they astronomical or terrestrial. Most telescopes fall into one of two main categories: refractor or reflector.[4] Refractor telescopes gather and focus light to make distant objects appear brighter, clearer, and larger.[5]

The Bible is like a telescope. A telescope doesn't make things appear larger than they really are. It magnifies our vision to see clearer and draws us closer to how big something already is. Spending time in God's Word magnifies our vision so that we see Him clearer and are drawn closer to Him. "Draw near to God, and He will draw near to you" (James 4:8).

Telescopes use a reflection of light to focus on distant objects. For us to have telescopic focus, we need light. God is light. So fixing our eyes on Him helps us focus more intently. The more we focus on Him, the clearer we will see Him. A focus on God brings perfect peace and turns life's chaos into peace. It literally sheds light on the subject.

I posed a question on social media, "What have you done to find peace that did NOT work?" The first response was prayer, but the Bible says that when we pray, we find peace. I have experienced it. But in my gut, I knew this response was somehow right. The next two responses cleared that up. One was redefining peace by ignoring circumstances or emotions in the name of being a strong Christian. We think we are supposed to do it ourselves and that as Christians, we should be strong. We pray, so we should have peace. But it's not a magic formula.

The next was giving those things to God, but then taking them back after we pray. I was reminded of Matthew 11:28-30, "Come to Me, all you who labor and are heavy laden, and I will give you rest. Take My yoke upon you and learn from Me, for I am gentle and lowly in heart, and you will find rest for your souls. For My yoke is easy and My burden is light." In simplicity, it's yoking up with Jesus to carry our burdens. Taking His yoke involves submission and obedience (because we love Him). Taking His yoke also means letting Him balance the load. We can't find peace when we try to do it alone. Just sitting down to pray when we are carrying a burden to pray, doesn't always bring peace. Peace comes when we share the burden in prayer and allow Jesus to help us carry it.

I can pray all day long, but if I don't acknowledge my limitations and problems, it's a farce. Isaiah 26:3 says, "You will keep him in perfect peace, whose mind is stayed on you, because he trusts You." When we focus on Him and when we praise Him, we have peace. When we praise God, it changes our focus to Him. We can't stay focused on problems or keep a negative attitude when we begin to praise and meditate on Him.

Taking a closer look at this verse, the word *stayed* is not just focusing on Him but much more. It is fully resting and trusting in Him. When I give Him my troubles and find rest, but then I take them back, I lose the peace.

Perfect peace is peace peace. No, that's not a typo. It's double the peace.

The Israelites were told to seek the peace of the city where they were held captive, for in that city's peace they would have peace. As stated earlier, we may need to pray for peace in a circumstance, not necessarily to be removed from that circumstance. We can hear God's voice from the midst of the fire as Moses did at the burning bush and again as God spoke to him on the mountain. Our hearts are set on fire, but there is a peace within.

Women in Scripture

Hannah was a woman in 1 Samuel who had no children, and she was provoked by another woman, Peninnah, who had many. Hannah's husband loved her. He asked her why she wept. He didn't understand her burden (anyone else been in a situation here your husband didn't understand?), so she poured out her heart to God in the temple. When the priest, Eli, saw her praying in distress, he told her to go in peace and may God grant her petition. Her face was no longer sad. She worshiped in the morning, and they returned home. Hannah came to the Lord with burdens and left with peace. Her problems were not immediately solved, but she had peace after pouring out her heart to God. She released her burden and left it there, trusting in the word of the prophet Eli.

During times of disappointment, we can allow ourselves to be provoked by others through their seemingly perfect lives. Social media shows more blessings than disappointments. Hannah's husband did not understand her sadness, but God did. He wiped away her tears and wants to wipe away our tears through His love for us. We must look to God, not the lives of others.

Jesus visited the home of his friends Lazarus, Mary, and Martha. While He was there, Mary sat at his feet to listen, but

Martha became distracted from listening by her concern over serving. The act of the women serving was normal, but this distraction of what was good and normal kept her from what was best, and she complained. Jesus said, "You are worried and troubled about many things. But one thing is needed, and Mary has chosen that."

One thing is needed. The word for needed means necessity. Hearing from Jesus is a necessity. Mary has chosen. Mary made a choice.

There are many good things we can do for God. But the one thing that is necessary is His Word. We sit at His feet and listen to what He has to say to us by going to His Word. Mary made a deliberate choice to do this. There were many good things that could be done, but only one was necessary. And she chose that one thing.

This doesn't mean we don't do good things for God. But the necessity is hearing His words to us. From that place, we are then released to move forward in what He has for us to do. We won't know what we are supposed to do of all the good things that are possible until we spend the time with Him to hear His words to us.

This story in my mind is a picture of peace versus turmoil. Both women loved Jesus. One chose peace and one was distracted by busyness. Being busy is not always wrong, but we start with peace so we know where to be busy.

An amethyst as a gem of fire is also our gem of peace. This seems like an oxymoron because in our world fire and peace seem opposite. Fire is a combustion that gives out bright light, heat, and smoke. Peace is freedom from disturbance. It is quiet and tranquility.

For Christians, they go together. An inner peace sets off a combustion of fire that gives out bright light, heat, and smoke that others see. They are drawn to the fiery peace within us that brings freedom from disturbance. It brings quiet and tranquility.

Our fight is not of this world. It has already been won. We can't stop fighting, but within the fight is peace. Within the fire is peace. While fire is many times thought of in terms of loss or destruction, it's the small things of fire that can be associated with peace. Like the flame of a candle burning or the flicker of a flame from a lantern guiding a path. It's when that small flame is set ablaze into a larger proportion that destruction can happen. But what if that larger flame could be used for good? What if it is used to get our attention to turn us back to God?

My prayer for all of us is that through burdens, disappointments, and captivity in our lives we would be drawn closer to God. We don't have to climb the shelves to see God. Instead, we look through the telescopic lens of His word to recognize His presence in our fires.

Treasure Hunt

Look up Matthew 5:14-16. What treasures of light do you find here? How do you shine for Him?

Emeralds of Hope

Introduction

A different phone call at work. Someone I didn't know. It was her—one of several hers over a short period of time that seemed to have gone on forever. She was the other woman. For some reason, she felt I needed to know the truth. He was breaking things off with her, and this was her version of "hell hath no fury like a woman scorned." He rejected her, so she needed me to reject him. Then again, I think a lot of what I picked up in the phone call was her sorrow. Her confession to me was a type of request for forgiveness. Was she the final straw? No. Just more confirmation of the hell I was living through.

A few weeks later she called again. This time to tell me that the first phone call was a lie. She was mad at him and wanted to cause problems, but she didn't want to be the cause of a divorce. She was sorry she had lied. Well, I had been stupid for a long time, but how stupid was I supposed to be? Why did she even know him in the first place? I knew this phone call was the lie, so I told her that her first call had nothing to do with our pathway toward divorce. I shared nonspecific things letting her know that if divorce were eminent, it had nothing to do with her. And it didn't. It wasn't her. It was him. It wasn't like she showed up on the scene and enticed him away. He went looking continuously. It wasn't her.

Once we spoke long enough for her to believe me, she changed her story again. She confessed that the first phone call was the truth, but he had told her it was her fault that divorce loomed on the horizon. She was sorry for my predicament and for any part she played, and yes, she knew she played a part somehow, just not as much as he led her to believe.

Where is hope when things seem hopeless? How could I discern the truth? This life gives no hope. Being grounded in the only real truth is what gives hope. I was not alone. I had an everlasting Father and a forever home. Where is your hope?

We have been born again to hope with a vision for our guaranteed future.

14

Born Again to Hope

"The steadfast love of the Lord never ceases; his mercies never come to an end; they are new every morning; great is your faithfulness. 'The Lord is my portion,' says my soul, 'therefore I will hope in him'" (Lamentations 3:22-24 ESV).

Have you ever lost hope? While editing this book, I lost hope—or rather, this chapter on hope. I spent several hours editing Chapter 14 on a Saturday. When I opened it early on Sunday morning, it was gone. Not only did I lose a chapter on hope, I felt devastated and started to lose hope itself. Sounds dramatic, I know, but how could I rewrite what took hours to edit and rearrange and change? I couldn't get it back. I had to leave it and come back later. In a way I had to grieve the loss of the time I spent and the resulting product that would never be the same. But if I trusted God with the words the first time, He could provide them again or even better. Since you are now reading this chapter, you know I found hope and rewrote it.

There are other things far more disappointing in life than losing a chapter of a book (though hard to imagine in the moment). There are times we need to grieve the loss of a person or a way of life. We grieve when our children leave the nest (or not). We grieve the loss of a marriage that falls apart. We grieve the loss, but we don't have to lose hope.

The following is a journal entry during a time of crisis when I felt lost and without hope.

> *Hopeless. An overwhelming feeling of loss. Loss of self. Loss of the will to continue. Loss of faith. Loss of strength. Loss of love. Loss of peace. Empty. No expectation. No control. Empty. It's hard to describe. No words do justice to this state of being. But in this state, there are no words, and there is no justice.*

> *Hopeless. Empty. Trepidation. Loss. Unknown loss. Not even knowing what was lost. Maybe trust. Maybe commitment and faithfulness. Maybe not a loss because maybe it was never there. Loss of an expectation and belief.*

> *Hopeless. The realization that the loss is not a loss because it was never real. Empty.*

> *Hopeless. The entrance of questioning is anything real.*

> *Hopeless. Darkness.*

> *I refuse to stay here. I will look for the promise of light in His light. I pray for His light to overtake the overwhelming darkness where I am living.*

Give ear to my prayer, O God, and do not hide Yourself from my supplication. My heart is severely pained and in anguish within me. I will call upon God, and the Lord shall save me. Evening and morning and at noon I will pray and cry aloud, and He shall hear my voice. Cast your burden on the Lord, and He shall sustain you. Create in me a clean heart, O God, and renew a steadfast spirit within me. Restore to me the joy of Your salvation and uphold me by Your generous Spirit. (Psalm 55: 1, 4, 16, 17, 22; 51:10, 12)

Emeralds

Emeralds are one of the four precious stones, but unlike diamonds, sapphires, and rubies which can be found in a variety of colors, emeralds are only green. They are the rarest of all the gemstones, and many cost more than a diamond. A myriad of websites link emeralds to growth, wealth, health, and eternal youth. Some even believe emeralds provide a truth potion or an aid to see the future. Emeralds were first mined in Egypt around 1500 BC where it was believed they stood for fertility and rebirth.[1] Early Christians valued the emerald as a symbol of resurrection. No better stone to represent our rebirth in Christ, our hope.

History and Hope

In 1922 scientists entered a hospital ward filled with diabetic children. Most of them were comatose and dying from diabetic keto-acidosis (DKA). A room full of parents sat at the bedsides of their children waiting for sure death. The scientists went from bed to bed and injected each child with a new purified extract called insulin. They brought a last-ditch effort for hope. As they injected the last comatose child, the first child started to wake up.[2] Can't you hear the gasps, the wonder of returned hope from the first child's parents radiating throughout the room to the last? One by one, all the children awoke from their diabetic comas. A room of death and gloom became a place of joy and hope. It took something to hold on to providing the hope they needed.

We hang onto our faith to give us hope. Faith is present. Hope is future. It begins with faith. They are intricately intertwined. Hebrews 11:1 says, "… faith is the substance of things hoped for." We see the hope of new life in a baby's birth. Spring flowers give us hope as the seeds dropped the previous year return to life. All new life starts with a seed. It is the source, the beginning, the nucleus. Sow, plant, scatter. Then comes the harvest. The birth, then the gathering home. A seed dies and is born again just as we die to our old life and are reborn in Christ.

"I hope so." We've all said it. When expectant parents say, "I hope it's a girl," it means they want a girl. When we try a new restaurant and say, "I hope they serve Mexican food," it means we want Mexican food. "I hope I pass the test" means we want to pass the test. Hope is something we desire and look forward to. To give up hope is to lose our desire.

Hope in Scripture is an expectation we can trust, not just desire. It requires something from us to make it possible. True biblical hope is a confident expectation. It's the opposite of discouragement. Hebrews 6:19 says, "This hope we have as an anchor of the soul," referring to our hope in Christ.

Born Again Unto Hope

Birth. It's the opposite of death, and in the face of mourning a loss, a new birth can give hope. His promise that life will go on. The birth of a child can give renewed hope to those who have experienced the loss of another. Birth is painful, at least for the mom. But we soon forget the pain once that little bundle of hope realized is placed in our arms.

My daughter was born via emergency C-section due to complications involving the umbilical cord wrapped around her neck. When it came time to give birth to my second child, we didn't know if this baby would be a boy or a girl. We hoped for (desired) a boy since we already had a little girl. In the one and only sonogram I had, this baby had legs crossed and was tucked in tightly. We didn't know. While we desired a boy, we would love either. We hoped for and looked forward to this child's healthy birth.

My doctor had let me know I didn't need to have another C-section since the complications of my previous delivery had nothing to do with me. But this time, they did. My labor had progressed to the point I was ready for an epidural, yet the hospital staff kept delaying. I repeatedly asked what was causing the delay and was told they had to wait until my doctor arrived. He was on his way.

They didn't quite tell me the whole truth. My blood platelets were too low, and there was concern about a normal delivery if I had passed this on to the baby. They were waiting for my doctor to arrive to discuss the options. Due to hospital policies, I couldn't have the epidural and ended up with another C-section under full sedation. It was scary. Depending on how low my platelet count dropped, I might not make it.

Waking up in recovery was like a double new birth. The birth of my son (our hope fulfilled), and the fact that I woke up.

I've heard the oxymoron, we are born to die. We aren't born to die, but to live. While our physical bodies will eventually wear out and die, the Bible talks about another birth where we are born to live and will never die. It is recognizing that in death, a new birth can give hope. In Jesus' death was sorrow, but in His resurrection, we have a new birth. It's in this new birth, we have hope.

To experience death is to have experienced life. You can't die if you haven't lived. We die to the sinful life we have lived and are born again unto hope that in this second birth, we will never die. God has begotten us again to a living hope through the resurrection of Jesus Christ. Jesus broke the chains of death and because He lives, we have a living hope, not a dead one.

Throughout the first chapter of 1 Peter, he tells us to rest our hope fully on the grace we have through Christ. We were not redeemed by corruptible things like silver or gold, but by the precious blood of Christ. This is the contrast of our physical jewelry box containing treasures of the earth from our first birth to our spiritual jewelry box containing prayer, faith, strength, love, peace, hope, and all the fruit of the Spirit. The contents of one will perish. The contents of the other give life. Our new birth is not of corruptible seed but incorruptible, which is through the word of God.

Throughout the Psalms is a cry for hope. This is where the prayer in my journal entry at the beginning of this chapter landed when I felt everything was hopeless. I prayed the Psalms. It's in God's Word that we find hope. And it's where I received and renewed my hope during that time of crisis.

Scripture Provides our Hope

Scripture was written for our learning, but we can't learn from it if we don't read it and hide it in our hearts. Through the patience and comfort we find in God's words, we have hope (Romans 15:4).

Let's look closer at the hope God gives as expressed in Romans 15:13.

> *"Now may the God of hope fill you with all joy*
> *and peace in believing, that you may abound*
> *in hope by the power of the Holy Spirit."*

The God of Hope

Where does our hope come from? God. He is the God of hope. Hope is expectation or confidence in what will be, and our hope is found in God, and God is found in His Word.

My children always brought me their needs. If a toy broke, they brought it to me to fix. They never doubted I could make it better. When they were toddlers, I began making their Halloween costumes. At first they were simple costumes made from T-shirts and paint. As my children got older, they assumed I could make anything. The costumes got more elaborate every year. One year they were Peter Pan and Tinkerbell. One year Snow White and one of the seven dwarfs. Another year Cinderella and Zorro. I was glad when they were finally old enough to stop asking for costumes. I don't think I could have done anything more difficult than the last few they requested.

In the same way my children were expectant and confident that their broken toys would be fixed and their costumes would be made, we can be expectant and hope in God to fulfill His promises. We can hope in God the same way our children hope in us. The only way we know what His promises are is to find them in His Word. He is our Father, and He is our God of hope.

Filled with Joy and Peace

God fills us with all joy and peace. True joy and peace are part of the fruit of the Spirit.

Galatians 5:22-23 lists the fruit of the Spirit as love, joy, peace, longsuffering, kindness, goodness, faithfulness, gentleness, and self-control. This fruit is not something we can strive to obtain but something produced in us through the Holy Spirit. John 15 gives a great example of fruit production. Branches of a fruit tree only bear fruit when the branch remains attached to the tree. If the branch is cut off, there will be no fruit. When we remain in Christ, we produce fruit. Just as 1 Corinthians 13 is not a recipe for love but a result of love as a fruit of the Spirit, the same is true of the other fruit mentioned in Galatians, including joy and peace. God, the God of hope, fills us with all joy and peace in believing.

In Believing

Hope is believing. We believe when we have hope. We trust for the future. If our God is the God of expectation and confidence, then we can put our full trust in Him. When I sit down in a chair, I trust it will hold me and not fall. That is faith. But when I trust for something in the future, that is hope. Faith moved forward.

My pastor, Craig Etheridge, spoke on Hebrews 11:1, "Now faith is the assurance of things hoped for, the conviction of things not seen. For by it the people of old received their commendation." Pastor Craig noted:

> What does that mean? That means in the Old Testament (by the way it goes through all of these great stories of Noah and Abraham and Moses and David), every single one of these guys when they were in their darkest place, in their darkest moment, instead of pushing God away (God, I don't trust You anymore); what they did do was they said, "Lord, I am going to trust in You." And when they did that, they found hope. Now listen, if you want hope, you have to do the same thing. You have to say, "Lord, I'm going to believe Your promise. Believe Your Word. And I'm gonna stand in a place of hope." It is then when He will fill you with peace and joy in believing.[3]

Abundance

We are filled with joy and peace so that we may abound in hope. This abundance means to exceed a fixed measure. It's having enough to spare. When we abound in hope, we overflow to others because we have more than enough and can share with others and stand in the gap for them. When you pour water onto a sponge, you can squeeze it and wring out the water. But if you immerse that sponge into a sink full of water and lift it out, there is more water than the sponge can contain, and it overflows onto whatever surface we place it. This is a picture of abundance.

The Power that Fills Us to Hope

It is by the power of the Holy Spirit that we are filled with joy and peace and abound in hope. When burdened, we can give up hope or look to the only hope. Hebrews 12:1-2 "Therefore we also, since we are surrounded by so great a cloud of witnesses, let us lay aside every weight, and the sin which so easily ensnares us, and let us run with endurance the race that is set before us, looking unto Jesus, the author and finisher of our faith, who for the joy that was set before Him endured the cross, despising the shame, and has sat down at the right hand of the throne of God." These verses epitomize our hope.

Moving Forward

The best way to move forward with our own lives is to help someone else move forward with theirs. When I'm stuck, it's usually because I'm empty and need to fill up in God's Word. As I'm filled with God's blessings, I must release to others. I must release to refill. The more I release, the more I can receive. It can flow out through a pinhole, or I can pull out the stopper and let it flow. The important thing is to remember how to refill. Being stuck can come from being empty and needing to be filled or from being full and needing to release.

In times of hopelessness, only God's Word brings hope. During the pandemic starting in 2020, there were days my hope felt threatened and shaken. The more I watched news reports of infection and death, the more I experienced fear. But when I immersed myself in God's Word, my hope was refreshed. Notice I said immersed myself in God's Word. Not a scripture here and there or a daily verse. An immersion in seeking God and searching for hope in His Word. Filling up on His promises over and above, and despite, the negatives in the world. Regardless of our circumstances bringing loss of hope, remember that we are born again to hope through our faith in Jesus.

Treasure Hunt

I want to give hope to others, and I'm sure you do also. The only place to find that hope to give is in the Word of God. Look up and study Psalm 119:49, 114, and 147. Where is the psalmist's hope? Where is your hope? Ask God to speak to you about how you can encourage hope in others.

15

The Emerald City

*"... looking for the blessed hope and glorious appearing of our
great God and Savior Jesus Christ" (Titus 2:13).*

A few years ago, I was sitting in the airport at 6:00 a.m. waiting
for a flight to Nashville at 9:20 a.m. Why so early? Well, Mr.
Wonderful dropped me off on his way to work. No big deal for
me. It gave me time to grab breakfast, relax, and write. As I get
older, I don't like the rush anymore. Then again, I've always
been one to arrive early. So, I sat looking out the windows
waiting for signs of the sunrise marking the light of another
day.

Sunrise. The light rising slowly and dispelling the darkness. Some days clouds move in and block the light, but it's
still there shining as bright behind the clouds as we see it on
a cloudless day. The light isn't diminished, just hidden for a
time. When the sun appears, the first ray of light gives hope

for the day ahead. Then the earth's rotation continues to bring a greater view of light. The only thing blocking the sun's light in the evening is the earth itself. The sun doesn't rise and set. That is just the appearance to us. It doesn't even move. In the darkness of night, the sun is just hours away from making another appearance as the earth continues to turn. The sun is still shining its rays on the earth somewhere. The earth's rotation brings the night and day.

When darkness clouds a time in our lives, we must remember that the light is still there. God's Word is what we use to break through the clouds and expose the light. His Word is filled with treasures shining brightly. God's Word is always there. We cannot escape His truth. We might turn away, but the only thing blocking us from His light is our own selves.

In the darkness of night in our lives, Jesus is waiting for us to turn back to the light of day. Our lives seem to spin in and out of darkness, but unlike the earth, we don't have to turn completely away. We can choose to stay facing the light. Yes, storm clouds will enter our lives and try to block our view. But the light from God's Word is strong enough to penetrate the thickest rain-filled clouds.

As we open God's Word and read the first ray of light, it pulls us in to a greater and greater exposure of His light in our life. I have certain "go to" verses when storm clouds enter my life, but the best light comes many times from just opening the Bible and reading anew, allowing His Spirit to guide me to the specific light for that day.

As I sat at the airport lost in thought, I glanced outside again. I didn't see the sun, but I knew it was there. The dark inky blackness had changed to gray. I could see images and planes and buildings. This was the beginning of the first rays of sunshine.

I normally think of a sunrise as beautiful, colorful rays of light. But it really begins with the ability to see things clearly before the colors appear. The darkness is dispelled before the beauty is revealed. So it is when we begin to read the Word. Darkness is dispelled before we realize the true beauty that awaits. We only need to watch for it and wait.

20/20 Vision

When I was young, I remember hearing the older folks say they couldn't see well enough to drive at night. I guess I'm getting older. Driving at night is not my favorite thing to do any more.

There are many scientific reasons why we see better in the sunlight than in artificial light. I experience this when sitting inside reading a book and needing reading glasses. But if I go outside, I no longer need those same reading glasses. It's like the sun has made the letters grow on the page. They don't really, but the entrance of sunlight makes my vision better.

In the same way, the entrance of "sonlight" makes me see better too. Psalm 119:130 says, "The entrance of Your words gives light."

Entrance in this verse is the word for opening, unfolding, or a doorway. Light here means to be illuminated or to light up. I picture a neon sign turned on outside a restaurant at night. God's Word illuminates the entrance to hope.

We see light referenced throughout scripture.

- At Jesus's transfiguration, Matthew 17 says His face shone like the sun.

- In Exodus 34, Moses's face shone after he had spent time with "THE" light.

- Ezekiel 43:2 says the earth shone with His glory.

- In Luke 2:9 the shepherds saw the light in the sky pointing to the newborn King.

- In Acts, Paul saw God's light on the Damascus road.

- When Peter was in prison, as told in Acts 12, a light shone when an angel of the Lord appeared to release him.

- Jesus said, "I am the light of the world. He who follows Me shall not walk in darkness, but have the light of life" (John 8:12).

According to Hebrews 11:1, hope is the evidence of things not seen. Hope is looking beyond our current situation to the future of what God has in store for us. It is the expectation of His promise. It is His light shining on our circumstances. The entrance of His Word opens the door of our heart, shining His light of hope on our circumstances and our disappointments. It shines the hope of tomorrow on our today.

Follow the Yellow Brick Road

Do you ever wonder if you're on the right path? Do you have a map? Where are you headed? Following God's path is our only hope in finding the purpose for which He created us. He leads us with His purpose for today to our eternal hope. We have a guaranteed future.

When we walk with God, He holds our hand. Scripture often refers to the right hand of God. It's a place of protection and a place of honor. A place of nearness to God and a place of power. Have you ever held a child's hand when crossing the street? Why? We hold their hand to protect them and help them learn because we love them.

> *"I, the Lord your God, will hold your right hand"*
> *(Isaiah 41:13).*

> *"Your right hand upholds me" (Psalm 63:8).*

> *"Your right hand will save me" (Psalm 138:7).*

Romans 8:34 says Christ is at the right hand of God making intercession for us.

Throughout the Old Testament, God leads and holds with His right hand. In the New Testament, Jesus sits down at the right hand of God. Today God stretches out His right hand to us through Jesus. Now when I read Scripture, I know that God is reaching out His right hand to lead me, guide me, and hold me through Jesus Christ. I can hold God's hand because of Jesus.

If I decided to take a road trip from Texas to Wyoming, I would study an online map before I left. I would also use the GPS on my phone or in my car, or maybe both, in case one wasn't clear in certain areas. With the online map, the GPS, the sun rising in the east and setting in the west, and the compass indicator in my car, I would feel confident in my ability to get to Wyoming. Every day of my trip, I would check my tools to make sure I was on the right road.

In life, the Bible is our road map. Many of us consult it but then take off on our own without it. This verse says that when we cease to hear instruction, we will stray from the words of knowledge. It's kind of like turning off that voice on your GPS.

First we quit listening to the voice, then we might quit looking at the screen, and before long we are lost.

When we quit studying our road map for life, we quit hearing instruction, and before long we stray from the knowledge needed to make a critical decision at the next crossroad in life. We must stay in God's Word, abiding in it and continuing to learn from it, or we will stray off the path He has for us. We can end up letting go of His hand when we still need fresh direction every day.

Just like a road map, take His Word with you on the trip of life. Allow Him to hold your hand and lead you. "Cease to hear instruction, my son, and you will stray from the words of knowledge" (Proverbs 19:27 ESV).

Work and Walk

"We are His workmanship, created in Christ Jesus for good works, which God prepared beforehand that we should walk in them" (Ephesians 2:10).

What is workmanship? It's the Greek word *poiema* meaning that which has been made or the works of God as creator. *Peripateo* is the Greek word for walk, but it also carries another definition which is to make due use of opportunity.[1]

Other references using this word for walk from Colossians tell us to walk fully pleasing Him, being fruitful; to walk in Christ; and to walk in wisdom, redeeming the time. Redeeming the time is making due use of opportunity. First Peter 5:8 says the devil seeks to devour in his walk, so I MUST walk with Jesus in mine. I am the workmanship of God to work for Him as He provides the opportunity.

Esther Stepped into Opportunity

> *"'For if you remain completely silent at this time, relief and deliverance will arise for the Jews from another place, but you and your father's house will perish. Yet who knows whether you have come to the kingdom for such a time as this?' Then Esther told them to reply to Mordecai: 'Go, gather all the Jews who are present in Shushan, and fast for me; neither eat nor drink for three days, night or day. My maids and I will fast likewise. And so I will go to the king, which is against the law; and if I perish, I perish!'" (Esther 4:14-16).*

Esther was willing to place her life on the line to save her people and give them hope for the future. She called for the Jews to fast, and by implication, pray. This made them part of the hope. In a similar passage in Joel, God issued a call to repentance, and just as in Esther ("... who knows whether you have come ... for such a time as this?"), Joel states, "Who knows if He will ... leave a blessing?"

> *"'Now, therefore,' says the Lord, 'Turn to Me with all your heart, With fasting, with weeping, and with mourning.' So rend your heart, and not your garments; Return to the Lord your God, For He is gracious and merciful, Slow to anger, and of great kindness; And He relents from doing harm. Who knows if He will turn and relent, And leave a blessing behind Him—A grain offering and a drink offering For the Lord your God?"*
> *(Joel 2:12-14).*

Verse 18 starts with the word "Then." The call is to return to God and "then" God will restore all that has been lost in not only a physical but, more importantly, spiritual restoration. God promises deliverance.

We can look back to Esther and her experience and have hope knowing that just like Esther, we were made for such a time as this.

Evidence

Mr. Wonderful worked in crime scene investigation for years. He worked with the evidence of things not seen. At a crime scene, something is always left behind. DNA, fingerprints, footprints, tire marks, blood spatter. While investigators may not have seen the crime, the evidence left behind allows them to see what was not seen.

"We do not look at the things which are seen, but at the things which are not seen. For the things which are seen are temporary, but the things which are not seen are eternal"
(2 Corinthians 4:18).

"For we were saved in this hope, but hope that is seen is not hope; for why does one still hope for what he sees? But if we hope for what we do not see, we eagerly wait for it with perseverance"(Romans 8:24-25).

The Nelson Study Bible says, "Hope is a constant expectation of an unseen reality."

"Nevertheless we, according to His promise, look for new heavens and a new earth in which righteousness dwells" (2 Peter 3:13).

Dorothy looked for the Emerald City in *The Wizard of Oz*, and we look forward to that new city also, new heavens and new earth where righteousness dwells. Even greater, we don't have to wait for heaven. We have a living hope today. "God ...

has begotten us again to a living hope through the resurrection of Jesus Christ from the dead" (1 Peter 1:3).

Mary

Mary, the mother of Jesus, called herself blessed among women. She had a willing heart, but she still needed hope. She would have had trepidation over telling Joseph she was pregnant and him not believing her. She would have had to deal with gossip and speculation culminating in the cruel death of her son. She found hope initially in her visit to Elizabeth. There was hope and encouragement when Elizabeth's baby leaped in her womb at Mary's arrival. She carried in her body the hope for all mankind. Mary's son didn't just give his life for family or country or the chosen of Israel. He gave His life for all, for you and for me. Mary's hope then is our hope today. Our hope is anchored in the truth of God's Word. Claim these promises of hope together with me. Read them out loud.

If God is for me, who can be against me?

When I draw near to God, He draws near to me.

I am God's workmanship. I am a child of God.

Jesus Christ is my hope. I have been born again of incorruptible seed.

He guards my heart. He supplies my needs. His grace is enough.

He cares for me. He is with me wherever I go. He will never leave me.

He restores my soul.

Greater is He that is in me than he who is in the world.

Christ in me is the hope of glory.

I am looking for the blessed hope and glorious appearing of Jesus Christ.

"Let us run with endurance the race that is set before us, looking unto Jesus, the author and finisher of our faith"
(Hebrews 12:1-2).

Treasure Hunt

Hope does not disappoint. Why? Look up Romans 5:3-8 and find more treasure here as you read His answers.

Notes

Chapter 7

1. *Merriam-Webster Learner's Dictionary*, accessed 2021, https://www.learnersdictionary.com/definition/friend.

2. Classic Senate Speeches, George Vest, Eulogy of the Dog, September 23, 1870, https://www.senate.gov/artandhistory/history/common/generic/Speeches_Vest_Dog.htm.

Chapter 8

1. Craig Groeschel, *#Struggles: Following Jesus in a Selfie-Centered World* (Grand Rapids: Zondervan, 2015), 178-179.

2. Ibid., 180-181.

3. Matthew Ervin, "The Ten Commandments Were Written on Sapphire Tablets From God's Throne," *Apple Eye Ministries*, June 15, 2014, http://appleeye.org/2014/06/15/the-ten-commandments-were-written-on-sapphire-tablets-from-gods-throne/

4. Louis Ginzberg, "The Project Gutenberg eBook of The Legends of the Jews — Volume 3" (Produced by David Reed), October, 2001 [eBook #2881] [Most recently updated: March 11, 2021], https://www.gutenberg.org/cache/epub/2881/pg2881.html.

5. Ibid.

6. Genesis 38:6-26

Chapter 9

1. "Ten Amazing Facts About Redwoods," *Hilltromper Santa Cruz*, accessed 2020, https://hilltromper.com/article/ten-amazing-facts-about-red woods

2. Matthew 15:8 and Isaiah 29:13

3. Jamieson, Fausset & Brown, . "Commentary on Psalm 107 by Jamieson, Fausset & Brown." Blue Letter Bible. Last Modified 19 Feb, 2000. https://www.blueletterbible.org/Comm/jfb/Psa/Psa_107.cfm

4. Henry, M. "Commentary on Psalms 107 by Matthew Henry." Blue Letter Bible. Last Modified 1 Mar, 1996. https://www.blueletterbible.org/Comm/mhc/Psa/Psa_107.cfm

5. "Sufficient." *Merriam-Webster.com Dictionary,* Merriam-Webster, https://www.merriam-webster.com/dictionary/sufficient. Accessed 2020.

6. "G714 - arkeō - Strong's Greek Lexicon (nkjv)." Blue Letter Bible. Accessed 2020. https://www.blueletterbible.org/lexicon/g714/nkjv/tr/0-1/

Chapter 10

1. Anne Sasso, "The Geology of Rubies," *Discover Magazine,* November 24, 2004, https://www.discovermagazine.com/planet-earth/the-geology-of-rubies.

2. Ibid.

3. Gary Chapman, *The Five Love Languages: How to Express Heartfelt Commitment to Your Mate* (Chicago: Northfield Publishing, 1992, 1995).

Chapter 11

1. W. E. Vine, *Vine's Concise Dictionary of Bible Words* (Nashville: Thomas Nelson Publishers, 1990), 174.

2. Advocare, Center for Specialized Gynecology, Hot Flashes, accessed 2020, http://www.advocarespecializedgynecology.com/getattachment/Services/Special-Conditions/Hot-Flashes.pdf.aspx

Chapter 12

1. Laura Schoker, "Your Body Does Incredible Things When You Aren't Awake," *Huffpost,* March 7, 2014 / Updated December 6, 2017, Accessed 2020,

https://www.huffpost.com/entry/your-body-does-incredible_n_4914577#:~:text=REM%20sleep%3A%20While%20bland%20dreams,does%20when%20you're%20awake

2. Ibid.

3. 2 Samuel 11 and 12

4. Cody Benjamin, "First victim to publicly accuse Larry Nassar: Grace and mercy 'will be there for you'", *CBSSports.com,* January 15, 2018, https://www.cbssports.com/olympics/news/first-victim-to-publicly-accuse-larry-nassar-grace-and-mercy-will-be-there-for-

you/#:~:text=I%20pray%20you%20experience%20the,that%20to%20 you%20as%20well.%22

Chapter 13

1. "Amethyst Healing, Meanings, and Uses," The Crystal Encyclopedia, Crystal Vaults, accessed 2020, https://www.crystalvaults.com/ crystal-encyclopedia/amethyst

2. Daniel 3

3. "G1515 - eirēnē - Strong's Greek Lexicon (nkjv)." Blue Letter Bible. Accessed 5 Jun, 2021. https://www.blueletterbible.org/lexicon/g1515/ nkjv/tr/0-1/

4. "All about telescopes: refractors, reflectors and more," *AstronomyToday*, accessed 2020, http://www.astronomytoday.com/ astronomy/telescopes.html#:~:text=A%20telescope%20is%20an%20 optical,combination%20of%20reflector%20and%20refractor

5. Refracting Telescopes, Las Cumbres Observatory, accessed 2020, https://lco.global/spacebook/telescopes/refracting-telescopes/

Chapter 14

1. Ten Things You Never Knew About Emeralds, *Diamond Rocks*, London, accessed 2020, https://www.diamondrocks.co.uk/magazine/ ten-things-you-didnt-know-about-emeralds/

2. Tanja, "On January 11th 1922, Insulin was First Used to Treat Diabetes," *Diabetes is My Life*, January 12, 2020, https://diabetesismylife.com/ on-january-11th-1922-insulin-was-first-used-to-treat-diabetes/

3. Craig Etheridge, MT 11-15-18, "Hope is Yours by Faith," First Colleyville, Colleyville, Texas, https://vimeo.com/298010123.

Chapter 15

1. "G4043 - peripateō - Strong's Greek Lexicon (nkjv)." Blue Letter Bible. Accessed 2021. https://www.blueletterbible.org/lexicon/ g4043/nkjv/tr/0-1/

Acknowledgements

Thank you to my husband, Mr. Wonderful, for your continued support and encouragement.

Thank you to my writing tribe from Living Write Texas. Your guidance and suggestions were invaluable.

Thank you to my writing partner, Lori Altebaumer. You kept me going and pushed me through to the finish line.

Thank you to my beta readers, Karen, Eileen, Deb, and Michele. You provided the feedback and encouragement I needed.

Thank you to my editor, Ann Tatlock.

Above all else, thank You Lord for Your Word that has restored all my shattered dreams and given me life. Thank You for providing the answers and direction for everything we need. I am forever thankful for Your faith, strength, love, peace, and hope.

About the Author

Donna Nabors is a wife to Mr. Wonderful, a mom, and a grandma to four boys and one girl. She works full time in the business world while fulfilling her love of writing at night and on the weekends. Donna is a follower of Christ, desiring to point other women to the hope found in God's Word. She is thankful for the Christian home where she grew up learning to read and study scripture and develop her relationship with Christ, as well as the amazing youth group where she was active and originally met Mr. Wonderful.

Her hobbies include reading, antiquing, and organizing. She often jokes that her life is in an Excel spreadsheet. Donna is the author of *Pearls: 5 Essentials for a Richer Prayer Life*, a contributing author in *Arise to Peace Daily Devotional*, author of *Mr. Blue Eyes* in Spark Flash Fiction, and several devotions. She blogs at www.donnanabors.com and would love to connect with you to speak at your next women's event.

Donna has been married to Mr. Wonderful for almost 20 years. They have four cat children: Kylie, Abbie, Munchkin, and Maggie. She is a proud native Texan currently living in Keller, Texas.